Praise for *Bending the Binary*

"Anyone who works with polarity as a magical principle will find something of value in *Bending the Binary*. Deborah Lipp dismantles the notion of magical polarity, shows how it works, and then puts it back together again, all to build a richer, more powerful, more inclusive approach to magic."

—Jack Chanek, author of *Qabalah for Wiccans*

"Deborah Lipp provides a much-needed guide to navigating the multifaceted concept of polarity in the 21st century. In this very thorough work, the author examines how polarity has all too often been reduced to an overly simplified gender binary and offers deeper insight which can be used to unlock a world of possibilities. Covering aspects of the Kabbalah, alchemy, Wicca, and more, this book not only includes philosophy but also gives practical rituals and handy tables of correspondence, making this an invaluable resource toward understanding a more complete vision of many forms of magical polarity and the gender spectrum."

—Michael Furie, author of *The Witch's Book of Potions*

"This book made me think and take time to unpack my feelings on various topics. Deborah Lipp's tone is sometimes that of a seasoned teacher and scholar of witchcraft and at other times it is her personal voice describing her journey as a queer woman. This book is a collection of observations, insights, and suggestions on ritual practices on the topic of polarity in magick…*Bending the Binary* will spark many conversations and that is an excellent thing."

—Ivo Dominguez Jr., author of *The Elements of the Wise*

"Deborah Lipp has articulated the essential insight that polarity is not synonymous with gender. The clarity of her thinking is breathtaking. The tension between opposites, which is resolved in their ultimate union, is central to many magical traditions, but linking this to gender has imprisoned those of us who do not fit rigid definitions. We've needed the binary to flex without

T0028363

destroying that kind of magic altogether. *Bending the Binary* accomplishes that feat. It's a long-overdue exploration of polarity in its rich diversity, creating an inclusive approach to magic…This is one of those groundbreaking books that will change the way we think and practice, essential on every bookshelf."

—Brandy Williams, author of *Cord Magic* and *The Woman Magician*

BENDING

THE

BINARY

© Marshall P. Reyher

About the Author

Deborah Lipp has been teaching Wicca, magic, and the occult for over thirty years. She became a Witch and High Priestess in the 1980s, as an initiate of the Gardnerian tradition of Wicca. She's been published in many Pagan publications, including *newWitch*, *Llewellyn's Magical Almanac*, *PanGaia*, and *Green Egg*, and has lectured on Pagan and occult topics on three continents.

As an active "out of the closet" member of the Pagan community, Deborah has appeared in various media discussing Wicca, including *Coast to Coast AM* radio, an A&E documentary (*Ancient Mysteries: Witchcraft in America*), television talk shows, and the *New York Times*.

As a pop culture writer, she's perhaps best known as the co-founder of *Basket of Kisses*, the premier *Mad Men* blog. She is also a contributor to *Mad Men Carousel* by Matthew Zoller Seitz.

In "real life" Deborah is a technology systems professional. She lives with her spouse, Melissa, and an assortment of cats in Jersey City, NJ, three blocks from a really great view of Freedom Tower. Deborah reads and teaches Tarot, solves and designs puzzles, watches old movies, hand-paints furniture, and dabbles in numerous handcrafts.

Follow her @DebLippAuthor on Twitter and Instagram.

BENDING

THE

BINARY

POLARITY MAGIC IN A
NONBINARY WORLD

DEBORAH LIPP

Llewellyn Publications
Woodbury, Minnesota

Bending the Binary: Polarity Magic in a Nonbinary World © 2023 by Deborah Lipp. All rights reserved. No part of this book may be used or reproduced in any manner whatsoever, including internet usage, without written permission from Llewellyn Publications, except in the case of brief quotations embodied in critical articles and reviews.

FIRST EDITION
First Printing, 2023

Cover design by Shannon McKuhen
Interior art by the Llewellyn Art Department

Llewellyn Publications is a registered trademark of Llewellyn Worldwide Ltd.

Library of Congress Cataloging-in-Publication Data (Pending)
ISBN: 978-0-7387-7262-2

Llewellyn Worldwide Ltd. does not participate in, endorse, or have any authority or responsibility concerning private business transactions between our authors and the public.

All mail addressed to the author is forwarded but the publisher cannot, unless specifically instructed by the author, give out an address or phone number.

Any internet references contained in this work are current at publication time, but the publisher cannot guarantee that a specific location will continue to be maintained. Please refer to the publisher's website for links to authors' websites and other sources.

Llewellyn Publications
A Division of Llewellyn Worldwide Ltd.
2143 Wooddale Drive
Woodbury, MN 55125-2989
www.llewellyn.com

Printed in the United States of America

Other Books by Deborah Lipp

The Elements of Ritual:
Air, Fire, Water & Earth in the Wiccan Circle
(Llewellyn, 2003)

The Way of Four:
Create Elemental Balance in Your Life
(Llewellyn, 2004; reissued by Crossed Crow Books, 2023)

The Way of Four Spellbook:
Working Magic with the Elements
(Llewellyn, 2006; reissued as *Magic of the Elements*
by Crossed Crow Books, 2023)

The Study of Witchcraft: A Guidebook to Advanced Wicca
(Red Wheel/Weiser, 2007)

The Ultimate James Bond Fan Book
(Sterling and Ross, 2006; currently self-published)

Merry Meet Again:
Lessons, Life & Love on the Path of a Wiccan High Priestess
(Llewellyn, 2013)

Tarot Interactions:
Become More Intuitive, Psychic & Skilled at Reading Cards
(Llewellyn, 2015)

Magical Power For Beginners:
How to Raise & Send Energy for Spells That Work
(Llewellyn, 2017)

The Complete Book of Spells:
Wiccan Spells for Healing, Protection, and Celebration
(Rockridge Press, 2020)

The Beginner's Guide to the Occult: Understanding the History,
Key Concepts, and Practices of the Supernatural
(Rockridge Press, 2021)

To my trans and nonbinary friends and family:
You have confused me and enlightened me.
You confront me when I get it wrong,
applaud me when I get it right,
and love me regardless.
I am a better human being and
a better magician because of you.

Contents

Figures

Charts

Acknowledgments

This book has had numerous lives, over many years, as I struggled to find a way to communicate my disparate thoughts about polarity. With each iteration, different people have helped me. Some of their contributions didn't make it to these pages as the book changed, yet I owe them thanks.

I should start with the late Niklas Gander. Fully ten years ago, I had the idea of a multi-author project that would have multiple queer voices. Niklas was one of those voices, and notes from our conversations all those years ago made it into this very different version. Niklas, a.k.a. Dr. Thomas Johnson, passed away in 2014 at the age of fifty-five.

The wonderful author Brandy Williams must have spent an hour on the phone with me out of absolutely nowhere, giving me all sorts of ideas and resources about the history of magical polarity. Both Lon Milo DuQuette and Richard Kaczynski contributed historical information about the O.T.O. Dr. Justin Sledge generously responded to my questions about the history of gender in alchemy, and Claudiney Prieto also helped me with his alchemy expertise. The iconic Rachel Pollack answered questions about her Doom Patrol character, Coagula. Sam Block was more than helpful about Hermetics, which is a tricky subject. My daughter, Ursula Rising, figured out the introduction to chapter 13.

Misha Magdalene offered a long and generous conversation about areas of the book that ended up being kind of sticky. I can't thank her enough. My daughter stepped up for that part as well, because no one can be blunt and ill-mannered with me, in just the best possible way, like Ursula can.

Jack Chanek was a constant companion, sounding board, and devil's advocate in discussions about Kabbalah and its relationship to polarity.

Other people who contributed thoughts about queerness, polarity experiments, and their generous humanity to this project include Darius Kenner, Sydney Weyl, Angela Zamora, William Seligman, and Paul Rösch.

Professor Spouse let me read to her and also graciously allowed me to use our relationship as an example in several spots. Seriously, you're sitting on the couch relaxing after a long day of teaching and grading, and your wife wants to randomly read you three paragraphs on Dion Fortune. I really owe her a lot.

My editor, Elysia Gallo, is always terrific, loved the book when it was merely an outline, and introduced me to Brandy Williams. She was supportive and helpful during a thornier-than-usual editing process.

Who Cares about Polarity Anyway?

I've been paying attention to the idea of polarity for a long time. I came out as a lesbian in 1976. I was initiated into a polarity-based Wiccan tradition in 1982. Over the years, those two things have bumped heads within me to a greater and lesser extent. My queer identity has gone through changes, as has my understanding of how it relates to magic. I'll circle back to my own story in a minute or two, but first let's talk about polarity itself.

In the occult world, polarity energy and polarity magic are discussed everywhere and defined hardly anywhere. We're told polarity is incredibly important, but we're not often told why or how.

For over a century, polarity has been described, in the world of Western occultism, as gendered and heterosexual. In fact, often it isn't even called *polarity*, it's called *gender polarity*, as if the two terms were identical. Occultism has almost entirely excluded or condemned same-sex love and same-sex magic. Polarity, we've been told, is both essential to magic and excludes all kinds of magical humans. It's been used as a tool and as a bludgeon. Queer occultists, if welcomed, have been told to "act as if" they were straight because, we've been told, gender polarity is innately tied to our gendered bodies. In other words, polarity has been defined in a way that is completely *gender essentialist*—a term we'll define shortly.

More recently, occult thinkers and authors have told us that polarity is a load of crap, that we should throw it away with other oppressive paradigms and not look back.

This is a book that stands at neither of those extremes. In these pages, we'll explore what it would mean to include polarity magic and also *be* inclusive. I have this idea that there's a baby in all that bathwater, and I'd like to save the little darling.

The Magical World

I learned the term *p-words* from Misha Magdalene, who picked it up from Laura Tempest Zakroff. In her book *Outside the Charmed Circle*, Magdalene describes p-words as "the various streams of modern magical (or occult) practice and the multiplicity of spiritual traditions falling under the headings of Paganism and polytheism."[1] We're going to get into some really interesting history later on, but for now let's just say that all of our Western p-word traditions, be they Neopaganism, Wicca, Thelema, Druidism, the Church of All Worlds, or the Church of I Made It Up Yesterday, all have some common ancestors and some shared energies. (Instead of p-word, I'll often just say occultism or magical people.)

Whatever label I use, someone won't like it—because people hate labels. But at a larger level, we can understand that our beliefs, practices, and values can be vastly different yet come from a shared root language, and that allows us to leverage a shared vocabulary. In other words, we can talk. What is said in these pages will strike each reader differently, in part because we all have different occult backgrounds (and in part because we're different individuals), but we can easily translate this information into our own magical languages. I might "speak" Wicca, but you have enough shared vocabulary with me that you can translate into Druidism or whatever.

My own magical background, which undoubtedly influences my writing both consciously and unconsciously, is primarily in Wicca. Over the

---

1. Magdalene, *Outside the Charmed Circle*, 30–31.

course of forty years in the Pagan and occult community, I've participated in a wide variety of rituals and experiences, attended classes, broken bread, and partied with just about every kind of magical person you can name, on three continents. My intention here is to write in a way that is welcoming to all of them/you/us.

Who Is This Book For?

Bending the Binary is for anyone who is interested in the subject of polarity in a p-word context. It is for anyone who has encountered the concept of polarity and wonders what that means to them personally, or what it means at all. It is for straight people and queer people, cis people and trans people. I don't assume who you are and what you know, and I may explain things you already know. You may be queer or trans or nonbinary, or all of the above, and be asking if polarity has any meaning to your magical practice. You may be the most heteronormative cisgender person in the entire world and be 100 percent comfortable with polarity as it was taught to you, and simply want to deepen your understanding of an important occult concept. Whoever you are, you are welcome.

The Queer World

Inevitably, this book must address queerness, the elephant in the room of any conversation about polarity. In these pages, queer identities will be front and center. Whether you identify as LGBTQAI+ or not, whether you know what all those letters stand for (we'll get to that), this is a book that welcomes you. I'll use *queer* here as an umbrella term covering and encompassing LGBTQAI+ identities because that's a comfortable word for me. I recognize that some people are uncomfortable with the word, which was once a slur,[2] but it's a word I embrace, as it fits *me*.

I started with the word *lesbian*, but once I'd married and divorced a man, that seemed like a weird word to continue to hold onto. Understanding that I was definitely not straight nor gay, I also didn't love *bisexual* or

---

2. The word *queer* was first used by the Marquess of Queensberry in 1894. See Perlman, "How the Word 'Queer' Was Adopted by the LGBTQ Community."

pansexual. None of those words ever nailed down exactly *me*. Let's be honest: there's a lot of gatekeeping in the LGBTQAI+ world. I've been made unwelcome in lesbian spaces because feminine gender expression is my happy place or because I date men. I've been told that there's no such thing as bisexuality or that I'm a "wannabe." Straight men fetishize bisexual women to such an extent that I've been known to withhold my orientation from men I date. None of that feels good or welcoming or free.

When the word *queer* came into use, it gave me permission to stop agonizing over the right definition. It allowed me to feel welcome in queer spaces, because however you define my orientation, it's a queer one. Being queer is good enough. It has been a liberating word for me, and I use it in that context.

The polarity magic I was taught comes from a world where everyone was assumed to be heterosexual and gender normative. Polarity didn't have to be questioned because it was "normal." The whole world was "obviously" binary, and a crucial descriptor of that binary was gender: everything in the universe was seen as male or female. Black and white, war and peace, winter and summer, sweet and sour—every possible pairing was a gendered pairing, and that was that.

The polarity I understand today is not that. We're going to be exploring binaries, and the power of binaries, and the transcendence of binaries. We're going to be exploring gender and how it interacts with polarity energy. We're *not* going to be making everyone stand in their gender-identified corners. We're going to be finding a power in this exploration that was, at one time, denied to those of us who are queer.

This increased power and understanding is something that can contribute to the magical life of anyone, whether or not you're part of the queer spectrum.

Identity

I am just one person. Writing as a woman, I cannot speak as a man or a nonbinary person. Being cisgender, I cannot speak with the voice of a transgender person. I cannot speak as a gay man, a straight person, a Christian, a person of color—a thousand different things that I am not. As a Wiccan, I cannot speak with personal experience and authority for other occult paths.

I acknowledge the limitations of any single author's voice. It is my intention to be respectful and inclusive of a huge range of experiences, but at the same time I write best when I write as myself and don't try to fake it. (Pro tip: Everyone does.) No one book can be the be-all and end-all, nor should it try. I will be inclusive, but I won't pretend to be someone I'm not. It's my hope that this book serves as an exploration and a conversation, not an instruction manual. I can't tell you how it's done, but I can tell you how it's been done in the past, and I can point to paths that look promising. I'm also actively engaged, every day, in connecting with and learning from my beloved friends and family who are trans, gay, straight, male, enby, asexual, and more. And yes, I am learning, which means I don't know everything and sometimes I'm wrong.

Because the author's voice is meaningful in terms of both my limitations and my subconscious bias, a bit more on my background is valuable.

I was initiated into the Gardnerian tradition of Wicca in 1982 and am also an initiate of the Minoan Sisterhood. I was, for quite a few years, a board member of Ár nDraíocht Féin (ADF), a Druid organization.

I am a Taurus with five planets in Earth signs. Perhaps for this reason, I value stability. The things I learned in the 1980s are things I value; I let go of them only slowly, and only when I fully understand why I'm letting them go. This book comes very much from that point of view—what's this polarity thing I was taught and is there anything of it I can keep?

The Gardnerian tradition is often thought of as a "conservative" or "old-fashioned" tradition. In some ways this is true. I am conservative about radically changing my tradition. I love it and I value its stability (five planets…). In other ways, it's ridiculous. I go to a couple of Gardnerian gatherings each year and looking around at my beloved co-traditionalists, with their tattoos, activism, polyamory, queerness, and anarchy, it's hard to see where the label came from. (We're not *all* any of those things. Certainly there are conservative, straight, monogamous Gardnerians—we're a diverse bunch.)

Labels that fit me include queer, bi, and femme. My pronouns are she/her. I am married to the magnificent Professor Spouse, who identifies as gay, butch, genderqueer, and nonbinary, and uses she/her pronouns. I am the mother of a lesbian trans woman. I am proudly Jewish and active in my synagogue. I am a late Boomer (okay), sometimes called Generation Jones.

I am the high priestess of a majority-queer Gardnerian coven that includes nonbinary members, a coven that uses, experiments with, and values polarity. (In my coven, we are comfortable with gendered language like *high priestess*. There are many covens today that prefer *priestex* as a gender-neutral term.)

Bending the Binary is my eleventh book. In the years since 2003, when my first book, *The Elements of Ritual*, was published, I have grown and changed. I mean, I should hope I've grown in twenty years! There are things I've said in print that have been gender essentialist and just plain wrong. Living a life in print means my past can be as visible as my present, but it's my honor to be corrected by critics and friends who have helped me become a better person, and I hope that is reflected in this volume.

What We're Talking About

In my 2007 book *The Study of Witchcraft,* I describe three broad types of Wicca: Traditional, Eclectic, and Radical Witchcraft. Roughly speaking, you can find Traditional Wicca in the works of older writers such as Gerald Gardner, Janet and Stewart Farrar, and Doreen Valiente, and more recently, Thorn Mooney. Eclectic Wicca is typified by the works of Scott Cunningham, and Radical Witchcraft by the works of Starhawk and others of the Reclaiming Collective. The approaches and styles of these types of witchcraft are very different, but I attempted, in that book, to identify a number of things that they all have in common.

At the time I suggested that the use of polarity as part of Wicca was shared across the board. It wasn't really universal then and is less so now. A number of thoughtful people have suggested, in books, talks, blogs, podcasts, and the like, that it's time to ditch polarity. If I agreed, there'd be no point in writing this book, so my bias here is obvious. I want to dig into the joys and the problems of polarity and see what's left when we explore it deeply and honestly. This applies not merely to Wicca, where I started, but also to the whole p-words complex, where many traditions explicitly use polarity and many others are influenced by its core concepts even when it's supposedly not there.

In the following pages, I'll explore polarity from a number of angles:

- What is meant by polarity in the occult and elsewhere?
- Where did the idea of polarity magic come from, and how did it turn into the sometimes limited, sometimes oppressive paradigm we often see today?
- What is the relationship of polarity to gender and orientation?
- What other kinds of polarity are there?
- What about nonbinary people and nonbinary magic?
- How can we work with polarity in ways that are respectful of the wide range of human experiences?

In section 1 we'll start by defining polarity and looking at the way the perception of polarity, dualism, gender, and that whole mess of ideas has arisen in Western occultism, how it started, how it has morphed, and where we are today. We'll explore the way that the binary gets transcended, even in the most traditional ideas about polarity. In section 2 we'll get into the practical side, talking about how different kinds of polarity might be experienced ritually, magically, and otherwise. Finally, section 3 will allow us to step into the future, and asks what's next with our new understanding of polarity.

If these subjects interest you, let's begin.

SECTION ONE
POLARITY
AND THE BINARY

Chapter One

Defining Polarity

If you've ever spent any time on the internet, you've surely noticed that people have the capacity to argue passionately about something without ever defining what they're arguing about. Whether it's gender, socialism, or classic movies, it helps to define your terms. Otherwise you're defending *The Breakfast Club* as a classic, but my definition of *classic* includes "made before 1975." We'll never agree, and we'll never know why we disagree.

Let's start with a loose, functional definition of polarity, and then get into what it means and (importantly) what it *doesn't* mean. In *The Mystical Qabalah*, Dion Fortune defines polarity as

> the flowing of force from a sphere of high pressure to a sphere of low pressure; high and low being always relative terms. Every sphere of energy needs to receive the stimulus of an influx of energy at higher pressure, and to have an output into a sphere of lower pressure.[3]

That's not a bad definition, but it's got a lot of woo-woo to it. Wendy Berg and Mike Harris's definition in *Polarity Magic* is more succinct:

> There must be polarity, the dynamics of relationship through which creative potential can be realized.[4]

---

3. Fortune, *The Mystical Qabalah*, 213.

4. Berg and Harris, *Polarity Magic*, 9.

That's a really good definition (even though it comes from what I consider a very flawed book), and it's one worth keeping in mind.

I'll add my own definition of polarity:

The presence of contrasting energies, forces, or conditions that attract one another, thereby generating power.

In the occult, the presence of polarity is perceived as a form of immense power, and the interplay of polar energies is seen in many traditions as a vital part of magic and/or ritual. It's also true that virtually every spiritual system that leverages polarity sees these contrasting or "opposite" forces as ultimately one.

An example is yin and yang. The black and white contrast shows duality, while the dots of opposite colors suggest that each contains the other and that they are not as "opposite" as they first appear. The fact that both colors are part of a single whole—a circle—shows their ultimate oneness. We'll return to this idea of an ultimate oneness later.

Yin and Yang

In Wicca, an example of polarity is the emphasis on the Goddess and the God. Wicca is often called duotheistic. Just as monotheism means there is one God and polytheism means there are many, duotheism is the belief in exactly two. To quote Dion Fortune, "All the gods are one god, and all the goddesses are one goddess, and there is one initiator."[5] Fortune's ideas are widespread in occultism, but it is in Wicca that this quote has most often been taken literally. It is typical in Wicca today to find covens or solitary practitioners who worship "the Goddess and the God," meaning two

---

5. Fortune, *The Sea Priestess*, 172.

transcendent beings who each have dominion over half of creation. The Goddess is the earth, the God is the sky, the Goddess is the moon, the God is the sun, and so on. This division of nature and reality into an interactive duality is exactly what Fortune meant, and speaks to the idea of a polarity energy that is constantly flowing throughout reality and therefore is accessible through occult means. That is, this energy is everywhere, and is accessible to those who have the knowledge to do so.

To be sure, there are a lot of variations of Wicca. My own tradition worships a specific goddess and a specific god. Their names are secret, so they are referred to as "the Goddess and God," but they are not generic "all Mother" and "all Father" beings. I tend toward polytheism and see my tradition's goddess and god as having primacy, but not exclusivity, in that tradition.

Polarity, as typified by Fortune's quote, has also been rightly seen as oppressive. In part it's oppressive because it's gendered. Female is seen as "negative" and "receptive" and male as "positive" and "active." The plot of Fortune's *The Sea Priestess* revolves around a powerful, ancient priestess who must nonetheless, because of her gender, wait for a worthy priest to "activate" her magic. Women get the short end of the stick in such divisions.

And even if the gender equation were somehow made more truly equal, classically described polarity seems to erase nonbinary people and nonbinary reality.

In p-word systems where polarity is considered a core functional element, we'll find that its energy is not dependent on a Victorian and gender-essentialist framing of those energies. As I've studied occult history, I've become more and more convinced that the oppressive aspects of polarity are a relatively recent phenomenon, and the concept itself, going back to antiquity, was more free, more pluralist, and allowed for more experimentation and diversity than the occultism many of us inherited.

We'll return to the subjects of gendered and nonbinary polarity. For now, let's note that the Wiccan "Lord and Lady" is a common example of polarity as expressed in Western occultism but is not the whole story.

Magical Partnership

One of the primary ways that polarity is supposed to be expressed in the occult is through magical partnership. That is, a couple working together are meant to generate polarity energy simply by the existence of their partnership as part of the work. Historically, the couple is often a romantic partnership and often of different genders, and these components have been considered necessary.

Versions of magical partnership are fairly ancient. For example, author Raphael Patai notes that "[in ancient Rome] the priest of Jupiter, the *flamen dialis*, had to be married; his wife was the *flaminica dialis*, the priestess of Juno."[6]

Balance and Completion

One idea of polarity that is both powerful and problematic is that it is necessary for completion and balance. Like a good diet, energies should be in balance. Both magically and interpersonally, there's the idea that polarity and partnership are necessary to ground the excesses of the opposite quality. Just as a pinch of salt can improve the taste of something sweet, each pole, by itself, is considered to be in need of its opposite pole to achieve its peak potential.

This is problematic when we view polarity as strictly existing in a couple, because it can create codependence. "I'm not complete without my partner/spouse" is not necessarily a healthy statement. Yet the need for balance is genuinely key in magic as well as psychology. When we work with the elements, we understand that we need intellect (Air) *and* feeling (Water) *and* energy (Fire) *and* grounding (Earth). Similarly, as we come to understand polarity, we'll see that each pole *in extremis* requires the other pole to be truly whole.

---

6. Patai, *The Hebrew Goddess*, 120.

The Spectrum

All polarities inherently imply the existence of a spectrum between them. The very fact that there is a North Pole and a South Pole implies the existence of an equator, and indeed of an entire planet. Black and white imply the existence of every shade of gray.

It's important for us to know that we can exist at a pole or along a polarity spectrum. Your gender might exist, for example, at the far end of male or of female, or somewhere along the spectrum between them (or elsewhere).

Magical Correspondences

In occult philosophy, pretty much everything is divided into correspondences. These are used in magic, ritual, and meditation, and most of them are polar. Everything corresponds to an element, to a sphere or path on the Tree of Life, and to a gendered pole. In this way, everything can be found to be in a polar relationship to something else. A "male" tree has polarity with a "female" tree, and magical tools can thus be made of different woods to express different polarities, since trees, like everything else in such a system, have gender. (This is in addition to whatever other correspondences the trees have that might be leveraged for their magical properties when a tool is made.)

What Polarity Isn't

One of the problems of discussing polarity is that people think it's all sorts of things that it isn't (not unlike socialism or classic movies).

Polarity Isn't Dualism

We'll be talking about dualism a lot, the idea that the entire physical, spiritual, or moral universe is of a dual nature. Ideas about polarity arise from dualism, but they're not the same thing. Dividing the universe into two camps (in *moral* dualism, those camps are good and evil) is dualism; deriving energy from dualism, or from any specific, individual duality, is polarity. You can leverage polarity energy whether or not you believe that the entire universe is dualistic in structure.

Polarity Isn't the Only Thing

I've read several essays that "reveal" that magic works just fine without polarity. These essays tend to follow a format like this: "I was taught that XYZ had to happen in ritual in order to generate polarity energy, but I did ritual without doing XYZ and the ritual worked anyway!" The essay invariably concludes that polarity is a bunch of bullshit and need never be used.

I've got one for you: "My mom taught me to add sautéed onions to mixed vegetables, but I made them without the onions and they still tasted good. Onions are therefore bullshit and don't have any place in food."

To be fair, Mama taught a lot of people that onions were required. There are definitely magical teachers in many systems to this day who insist that magic *cannot* work without polarity. I'm here to tell you they're wrong.

Polarity is an ingredient in magic and ritual, but there are other ingredients. You can live a full and interesting occult life without ever working with polar energies. It's true that some systems are structured heavily around those energies, and some consider it a necessary linchpin of the work they do. In other systems, polarity doesn't exist as a concept, and in still others, it's an option.

Polarity Isn't Romance

There's an idea in some magical systems that the way to "do" polarity is by being in love with the person you work with magically. If we go back to our definition, it's easy to see that a romance usually does contain both contrast and attraction. So, sure, romance has polarity in it, but that doesn't mean polarity *is* romance. You can work with these energies even if you don't have or don't want a life partner.

Polarity Isn't Gender

Light and dark. Earth and sky. Sun and moon. Birth and death. Male and female. Dualism tells us that the universe is binary and therefore everything, *everything*, can be divided into white chess pieces and black chess pieces, and that's your team, no switching sides, end of story. Which means that, assuming you identify as one binary gender, you're stuck with all its other characteristics: no solar energies for you, woman!

Let's unpack this and say that gender has been used as a convenient descriptor for dualism but that the ideas associated with each gender are culturally driven. Let's further say that there is room, even in a discussion of "twoness," for more than two genders. We'll get back to that.

Polarity Isn't Heterosexual Intercourse

Again, attraction (optimally for most people) and contrast exist during sex, and energy is generated. That's awesome. The part that isn't awesome is how the idea of "contrast" is used as a secret homophobic gotcha—this happens both outside the realm of the occult and, too often, within the occult. Look, there's an outie and an innie, therefore *it's natural*, therefore *this is how it should be*, and so on, and so on. I hope no one needs to read an explanation of why that is homophobic; it should be obvious that *many* things are natural. The animal kingdom is full of homosexual behavior and, indeed, all sorts of sexual behavior other than intercourse.

If it so happens that you enjoy having sex in this particular way, and you raise energy that way, hurray. But like romance, sex is just an option in polarity work, not the definition of it.

Polarity Isn't Fertility

Just as people have conflated polarity with heterosexual intercourse, they have also conflated it with fertility, a potential by-product of heterosexual intercourse in most animals. This belief is exacerbated by the fact that writers of the nineteenth and twentieth centuries would often say, coyly, that something was a "fertility" ritual when they meant that it was phallic or yonic, or just plain sexy.

In fact, fertility magic is its own thing, sometimes accompanied by polar magic, sometimes not. We'll learn, when we talk about electricity, that you can energize something by placing it between poles. During intercourse, the "something" might be an ovum. Or not.

Lots of fertility magic has nothing to do with polarity, or even hetero-sexuality. Blessing the crops with a corn dolly, for example, is neither polar nor particularly sexy. Further, the idea that polarity equals fertility is con-tradicted by the idea (often propounded by the same teachers) that polarity is part of every ritual and is present in all male/female partnerships, even asexual ones.

We'll talk more about all of this in the next chapter.

Some Facts and Some Science (Not Too Much of Either)

For millennia, polarity has been described as "natural" and, as science developed, "scientific." Victorian-era occultists were particularly fascinated by electricity and the way that emerging scientific knowledge could sup-port or explain occult phenomena. In addition, science is one of the fun ways that society in general, sometimes including the occult community, has been oppressive of queer people. So before we go any further, let's look at a little bit of actual science about polarity and about queerness, and see what it tells us about our occult understanding.

Electricity is energy created by the existence of charged particles: elec-trons and protons. (Particles without a charge are neutrons.) Protons have a "positive" charge and electrons have a "negative" charge. Let's pause to note that the positive/negative designation is completely meaningless. Benjamin Franklin coined it based on his subsequently disproven theory of electricity. There's nothing "positive" about a proton. Charged particles could just as easily be designated "type A" and "type B."

Charles-Augustin de Coulomb, an eighteenth-century French physi-cist, stated that like charges repel and unlike charges attract. An electron surrounded by other electrons is repelled by them and will seek to move toward any nearby protons. (Electrons are lighter than protons; therefore they do most of the moving.) Equal amounts of protons and electrons tend to neutralize each other.

Now let's look at how batteries work. A battery is a closed system that uses the attraction of unlike forces to create and capture electricity for some purpose. In a battery, a chemical reaction causes a buildup of electrons in the *anode*. Since electrons repel one another, they move—toward the protons in the *cathode*. Upon reaching the cathode, the electrons are neutralized.

Batteries produce power by placing something that uses the electrical charge between the anode and the cathode. As the electrons move from anode to cathode, they move through the (flashlight bulb, toothbrush, vibrator, etc.), charging it. A battery is dead when the chemical is used up—no more reaction, no more electron buildup, no more charge.

Since this is the metaphor that has been used for centuries to explain magical polarity, let's compare and contrast.

The Occult Metaphor of Electricity

Dion Fortune's *The Esoteric Philosophy of Love and Marriage* is a little-known but highly influential[7] book that is essentially an extended metaphor about how electricity and the life force are alike, and what that means about sex. She says:

> It is well known that for electricity to become active, it must flow in a circuit....So it is with the life-force. It flows into each monad from the Divine source, and, having passed through that monad and energised it, flows forth into circumambient space; then...it is finally reabsorbed by the Divine....If, however, it is desired to perform any work with this force, it must not be allowed to radiate into space and so become unavailable; it must be concentrated into a definite channel, and...be converted into pressure and thus made a source of energy.[8]

Fortune then goes on to describe two types of "monads," with different energy flows, then defines those monads as negative/female and positive/male, and describes the magical function of sex as the creation of a circuit of life-force energy for the purpose of magical work, which she calls "cosmic

---

7. By which I mean, many, many commonplace ideas in the occult can be traced back to this book, yet few people have read it or realize it is the source of such ideas.

8. Fortune, *The Esoteric Philosophy of Love and Marriage*, 40–41.

sex, or polarity."[9] This is polarity magic in a nutshell, as understood by magicians and occultists of all stripes.

Fortune's definition seems to contradict my statement that polarity isn't heterosexual sex. That's partially because Fortune was wrong about a lot of stuff (albeit fascinating, and important, and really informative about the stuff she got right), but also, several pages later, Fortune herself says, "Union upon the physical plane need not take place, and, in fact, will not take place while the life-forces are being used upon other levels."[10] In other words, no hanky-panky.

She adds:

> The Cosmic Tie is a union that is entered into by two individuals for the purpose of performing certain occult work that can only be carried out by two units functioning in polarity; it has nothing whatever to do with love or attraction as ordinarily understood.[11]

How Electricity and Occult Polarity Are Alike

Both occult polarity and electricity understand that unlike forces attract, and that this attraction is a source of energy. Fortune explicitly describes intercepting a natural circuit prior to the point where it will tend to neutralize—just as your toothbrush does.

Both science and the occult understand that these forces as unlike but complementary—not opposites.

How Electricity and Occult Polarity Are Unlike

The occult tends to pay no attention to the idea of like forces repelling. While there is plenty of homophobia in the history of the occult (including some virulent stuff in Fortune's work), the "repulsion" force is mostly ignored, and there's no occult history of using it as an energy source.

---

9. Fortune, *The Esoteric Philosophy of Love and Marriage*, 41.

10. Fortune, *The Esoteric Philosophy of Love and Marriage*, 76.

11. Fortune, *The Esoteric Philosophy of Love and Marriage*, 77.

In a battery, we definitely see that repulsion is as necessary as attraction—electrons are driven *away* from each other as they are driven *toward* protons. There's no standard analogous magical act, and it's a rich area worth exploring.

Further, the occult and science view the moment of energizing differently. Electrons energize as they move toward a proton; upon arrival, they neutralize. In magic, a common method of polarity work is to hold the unlike forces apart as long as possible and then bring them together, creating energy and immediately releasing it, at which point the work is complete and the force can be grounded/neutralized. Again, this difference creates a ripe field for exploration and experimentation, moving the magical work to different points in the connection of the polar forces.

The Creation of Life

Theories about the origins of life on earth are suggestive of polarity as well, including the theory that electricity itself was the catalyst. To quote one scientist, "Electric sparks can generate amino acids and sugars from an atmosphere loaded with water, methane, ammonia and hydrogen…[suggesting] that lightning might have helped create the key building blocks of life on Earth in its early days."[12] Or the catalyst might have been hydrothermal vents, generating immense heat in the ocean.

What's clear is that a catalyst is required. *Something*—heat, electricity, crystals—acted to move molecules toward one another in a way that created life. The idea of polarity-as-catalyst is a powerful one, transcending gender, sex, and the human body entirely.

In an essay about polarity in Wicca, Lynna Landstreet sees this as critical. Describing the Wiccan ritual sometimes called the "symbolic Great Rite," in which the ritual blade (athame) is plunged into a goblet of wine, she says:

> That, to me, is the true Great Rite, of which all other enactments, sexual or not, are merely symbolic. That moment of lightning striking

---

12. Choi, "7 Theories on the Origin of Life."

the primeval sea to create the first living organism is what I see when the athame touches the wine.[13]

Defining Sex Stuff

We're not going to be able to get very far unless we pause to define a few things that can be confusing: sex, gender, gender identity, and sexual orientation. All of these can contain polarity,[14] and all have been (wrongly) defined *as* polarity. Misunderstandings about the sex stuff have been used oppressively in regard to magical polarity.

What Is Sex?

Let's look at what a number of biologists have to say about the matter. The idea that sex is determined by the presence of XX or XY chromosomes "is great for teaching the importance of chromosomes but betrays the true nature of biological sex."[15] Chromosomes can be incredibly complicated.[16] Even setting that aside, your chromosomes might not agree with your hormones, which might not agree with your body shape, or with something known as "cell signaling." Some of these can be nonbinary. "You may be genetically male or female, chromosomally male or female, hormonally male/female/non-binary, with cells that may or may not hear the male/female/non-binary call, and all this leading to a body that can be male/non-binary/female."[17] The math is such that if every different combination of chromosomes, hormones, morphology, etc., was defined as a sex, then the number of sexes would be nearly infinite.

Scientists study this because getting sex right means getting laboratory results right; it means getting medications, dosages, and treatments right.

---

13. Landstreet, "Alternate Currents: Revisioning Polarity."

14. All but one, anyway. I don't see a lot of inherent polarity in orientation, and I haven't provided any working ritual examples of orientation polarity.

15. Sun, "Stop Using Phony Science to Justify Transphobia."

16. Montañez, "Beyond XX and XY."

17. Open Ocean Exploration (@RebeccaRHelm). "Friendly neighborhood biologist here. I see a lot of people are talking about biological sexes and gender right now...."

There are people who want to say that studying sex is "trendy," but the fact is, studying sex is necessary and always has been.

Short answer: biological sex is a spectrum, even in lab rats. Male and female are rough buckets into which most people and other animals fit, but there are more intersex people in the world than there are redheads. We perceive sex as a binary, but the better scientists get at studying it, the less that seems to be true.

What Is Gender?

For decades, it's been common to say that "sex" is what your body is and "gender" is how you identify yourself. By these definitions, a transgender person is someone whose self-perception of gender doesn't match their body; that is, a trans woman is someone who was born in some version of a male body (given the complexity we just described, let's say a visibly male body, or a body with a penis) but identifies or perceives herself as a woman.

However, we can also talk about sex as having multiple definitions. To quote one scientist of human sexuality, "chromosomal sex; gonadal sex; morphological sex and related secondary sex traits; and psychosocial sex or gender identity."[18] In other words, gender identity is one aspect of sex. Scientists don't really want to separate gender into its own thing because that, itself, is a binary, "sex-equals-biology, gender-equals-society."[19]

But to get out of the weeds, gender can be understood as the perceived social aspect of sex. A person can identify as a man, a woman, as genderqueer, as nonbinary (enby is a term comfortable for many, but not all, nonbinary people), or as some other term. We're just now inventing terms, so they're all kind of in flux, and some of them could easily disappear from usage, while new ones could arise.

My gender is what I know myself to be. It is part of my authentic self. It may or may not be the same as what you'll find in my panties.

18. Herdt, *Third Sex, Third Gender*, 30–31.

19. Herdt, *Third Sex, Third Gender*, 52.

What Is Gender Expression?

Simply put, gender expression is how you show your gender to the world. Obviously, not everyone who identifies as a woman is interested in showing the world an ultra-feminine identity. Second-wave feminism was adamant that a woman was not the display of womanhood. Makeup and heels don't make you a woman. We've now gotten to the point where we understand gender expression in a more nuanced way. A man can identify as a man and enjoy dresses and makeup (see: Billy Porter). A woman can be confident in her identity as a woman and choose to eschew traditional gender expression. This *includes* trans people, who are sometimes expected to be super performers, as in, trans women are expected to go all out with makeup and girlie clothing, and trans men are expected to be all boots and flannel, all the time. It's not that simple. Indeed, nonbinary people don't need to wear strictly gender-neutral clothing, and often enjoy the most florid and beautiful getups. Music star Janelle Monáe, for example, is nonbinary, but her clothing and makeup appear quite feminine. People have no obligation to offer you a gender expression that gives you an easy shorthand understanding of their gender identity.

What Is Gender Essentialism?

Gender essentialism treats gender as an immutable trait. It is "the belief that a person, thing, or particular trait is inherently and permanently male and masculine or female and feminine."[20] Most people will attempt to tie gender-essentialist beliefs to biology—you "are" your chromosomes, or your genitalia, or some other physiological characteristic.

In magical communities, gender essentialism often gets a twist: people "are" whatever gender their *energy* is. A gender-essentialist coven, for example, might accept a transgender member on the basis that their lived gender matches their energy; a trans woman assigned male at birth can be accepted as a woman because her energy is essentially female. But such a group still ties gender to polarity in a one-to-one, dualistic way, generally

---

20. Abrams, "Gender Essentialism Is Flawed—Here's Why."

stating that feminine energy is passive, receptive, and fluid, while masculine energy is active, directed, and rigid. The Farrars say that "what matters is…psychic *gender*."[21]

On the other hand, gender essentialism is sometimes used as a justification for transphobia in the magical community. The belief that there's some essential and indelible energetic quality of the gender a person was assigned at birth is used to excuse refusing to accept trans people in their authentic genders.

I'm now going to tell a personal story that doesn't exactly cover me in glory. I got it wrong and it took me a long time to realize it.

In the 1980s I was a guest at a ritual, and it wasn't much of a ritual. I went home complaining about it. It felt empty, it was dull, and I finally said, "It felt like there was no priestess there." (It was a gender-polarity based ritual.) The person I'd attended the ritual with responded, "You know that [Priestess] is trans, right?" I did not know that, and I don't recall if I'd even met a trans person before that night.

Based on that experience, I developed an elaborate personal theory of gender and gender essence. There was no priestess in the ritual because she lacked some essential "woman" quality that comes with a uterus, or with being raised as a girl, or I don't know what. She was a woman. I was happy to accept her as a woman and I didn't think of myself as at all transphobic, but also, in some magical or energetic way, I was sure that she *wasn't* a woman and that my experience proved it.

It took me years to ask myself: What if she was just a bad priestess? Or a good priestess having a bad night? What if it was just one night, one ritual, and one experience?

I've been at a lot of rituals, and a number of them have been empty and dull. I don't question the gender of a cis priestess when that happens, so why should I question the gender of a trans priestess?

The essence of bigotry is using too small a sample size to draw a too big conclusion, and only doing that when confronted with a marginalized group. Many racists draw conclusions about crime only when the criminal is Black. Many sexists draw conclusions about emotionality only when the person being emotional is a woman. And I drew a conclusion about gender only because I knew the person was trans. I thought I was being insightful, but I was being a bigot. In other words, I was being gender essentialist.

Gender essentialism permeates Western culture, and indeed every culture. (While many Indigenous cultures have had broader and more inclusive understandings of gender, through colonization this nuance was often stripped away.) As we dive into history, we'll see the ways it has been incorporated into occult thought. But modern p-word practices are influenced not just by occult history but also by social context generally and by other social movements.

In the United States particularly, Pagan spirituality developed side by side with second-wave feminism and the women's spirituality movement, both of which could be profoundly gender essentialist. You can see this gender essentialism, for example, in ideas about a prehistoric matriarchy, where goddesses were worshiped and the world was more gentle and nurturing.[22] The reverent remembrance of this time has permeated a lot of p-word thought, despite there being no archaeological evidence of such a matriarchy. While it is true that not every society in history has been patriarchal, the thrust of the "prehistoric matriarchy" belief is that rulership by women has some essential difference from rulership by men—an essential difference in gender. These ideas were the norm in many p-word communities from the 1970s through the 1990s and later.

What Is Orientation?

The word *orientation* is used to identify erotic or romantic inclination, such as gay or straight. Big surprise: orientation is also a spectrum! Orientation is not the same as sex or gender. You can be a gay or straight transgender person, for example. In addition to gay/lesbian or straight, orientations that exist are bisexual (attracted to more than one gender), pansexual

---

22. See Eller, *The Myth of Matriarchal Prehistory*, for the best analysis of this concept.

(attracted to any and every gender), and asexual (not experiencing feelings of sexual attraction—called *ace* for short).

Orientation can shift based on how it's defined. Some people are erotically bisexual (they'll sleep with multiple genders) but romantically gay or straight (they'll only fall in love with one gender). And that adds *aro* (aromantic) to the orientation list.

The changing definitions of and understanding around gender and orientation are personal to me. I've spent my life with changing definitions of my orientation. Prior to using *queer*, I have at various times used *lesbian, bisexual,* and *heteroflexible.* (At other times I just kind of refused to answer the question because it felt too complicated.) Indeed, definitions of words I've used have changed as well. *Bisexual* used to mean "attracted to two genders," as if there were only two. Some people use *pansexual* to mean "attracted to humans regardless of gender," or, as someone once described it to me, "I'm attracted to spirits, not bodies." When I first heard that, I thought, "Oh, that's not me." I'm definitely attracted to bodies and to gender. It's not accurate to say I don't care what's in your pants. I do care. I just like more than one of the possible answers (and there are gender identities I'm not particularly attracted to).

My beloved Professor Spouse identifies as *genderqueer*, but that's a word she chose before *nonbinary* was in common usage. She now uses both, as well as *butch.* The language, then, is not just theoretical in my family.

What's with the Alphabet Soup?

LGBTQIA+ means:

Lesbian means women who identify as oriented toward other women. This began to be separated from *gay* in the 1970s, when gay women noticed they were often explicitly or tacitly excluded from gay spaces.

Gay typically means gay men—men who are oriented toward other men. It can also be a synonym for *homosexual* and mean both gay men and lesbians.

Bisexual, as defined above, means oriented toward more than one gender.

Transgender is sometimes used to include *nonbinary* and sometimes not. A trans person is someone who identifies as other than the gender they were assigned at birth. Other acronyms you'll see are *AFAB* or *AMAB*, meaning assigned female at birth or assigned male at birth. Trans people prefer AFAB and AMAB to the prior terms, which were *MTF* and *FTM*, meaning male-to-female and female-to-male. Many trans people assert that they were *never* the gender they were assigned at birth. Thus, a trans woman might say MTF is inaccurate because she was never M. Some trans people are not comfortable with the terms AMAB/AFAB either, for the simple reason that no one really needs to know what sex they were assigned at birth. We use the terms in my group for parents of transgender adults, but there, as parents, we often talk about birth, babyhood, and growing up, as well as our adult children in their authentic gender today, so in that specialized circumstance the distinction is helpful. I don't want to say something awkward and inappropriate like "when my daughter was a little boy," so I would instead say "when my AMAB daughter was little"—that conveys my meaning without misgendering her.

Nonbinary people can accurately say they are not the gender they were assigned at birth. For that reason, some nonbinary people also use the word *trans* to describe themselves. Others do not. Some people use *trans* only to refer to those who transition, who undergo a process of changing gender, which may or may not include medication or surgery and generally also includes things like changing one's name and whatever identity markers are accessible for change.

And some trans people might continue to identify as nonbinary. I know one trans woman who has shifted from he/him to they/them to she/her, and has a female gender expression while continuing to identify as nonbinary. Her AFAB partner identifies as trans and nonbinary as well, and has begun taking gender-affirming hormones while continuing to use they/them pronouns. This isn't at all uncommon.

Nonbinary, like *bisexual*, is a bit of an umbrella term. *Gender-queer*, *gender-fluid*, *agender*, and *gender flexible* are all variations of *nonbinary*, or may be considered so by people who identify in that way. Many nonbinary people don't perceive themselves as existing on a spectrum "between" male and female, which still seems to define them by reference to "male" or "female." It's fair to say that gender is a spectrum, and that most people perceive male and female as the extreme ends of that spectrum, but we shouldn't be forcing everyone to fit into that particular spectrum against their will. There are, after all, other spectrums. Again, terminology is changing, but it's helpful to know that not every nonbinary person has the same understanding of their gender as every other nonbinary person, which is, I think, as it should be.

Queer means somewhere on the spectrum of any or all of any of the other letters. Sometimes Q stands for "questioning," meaning not sure yet.

Intersex means the biology of your sex is complicated, perhaps because of chromosomal anomalies or something morphological (meaning your body shape). The word *hermaphrodite* is considered a slur by many intersex people.

Asexual people don't experience or rarely experience sexual attraction and have no desire for sexual relationships, although they may experience libido. *Ace* people may or may not also be *aromantic* (having no desire for romantic relationships). Like non-binary, *asexual* is an umbrella term that includes things like *demi-sexual* (experiencing sexual attraction only when an emotional bond exists) and *graysexual* (experiencing sexual attraction very rarely). Terminology here is emerging and evolving.

✛ The plus sign is used to communicate that there are more kinds of people in the world than the ones identified here.

Why Are We Talking about This?

As we proceed, we're going to toss around terms like *gender polarity* and *sex polarity* and *sexual/erotic polarity*. Most people assume they know what is meant by those terms, but most people learned biology in middle school and then stopped. So this little bit of education will help us later on.

Journal/Discussion Prompts

Throughout this book, there will be journal/discussion prompts. This will help you place yourself in the picture. Each will ask questions about your experience of the subjects raised in that section. These prompts can be used for fruitful discussion in your magical group (if you have one). They can also be part of a book discussion or a subject for a Pagan moot or meetup. If you are a solitary practitioner, you can use these questions for journaling and/or meditation.

- Do you worship "the Lord and the Lady"? How do you perceive them? Do you think they are heterosexual?
- Do you work with a magical partner? If so, how do you perceive the energy of partnership?
- What magical correspondences are a normal part of your practice? Are they polar?
- How does your magical practice treat sex and gender?

Chapter Two

One, Two, Three

Now it's time to talk about the ways in which polarity plays out not in a black-and-white world but in the world in which we live: a rainbow world of infinite color.

Polarity energies can exist wherever we find "twoness," but certain kinds of twoness seem to be more fundamental, and more universal, and therefore have more potency in magic and ritual. We know that historically gender has been treated as a universal and fundamental binary, and we know we want to move away from that and see what else is going on. It turns out there's a *lot* going on. (In chapters 4 and 5, we'll explore the history, especially p-word history, in more depth, and see how some of these ideas arose.)

The Binary: Twoness

Our brief foray into the science of electricity showed us that energy is generated on a continuum of attraction/repulsion. Energy becomes usable, and indeed magical, when attraction is held at bay in some way. An electron is attracted to a proton, but something stands between them. The electron's energy is intense in its headlong rush to the proton, but upon arrival it is dissipated (neutralized). Something needs to intercept the energy before that happens.

I was trained in a coven in which gender was assumed to be the *sine qua non* of polarity energy. In fact, gender was treated as far more important than any sexual or romantic energy. The assumption in those days was that "gender energy" was generated from the body in a steady thrum. To leverage polarity energy, we did everything, as much as possible, in alternating gender order. If everyone was to approach the altar, a man would be followed by a woman. If one man wanted to hand a magical tool to another man, he'd hand it to a woman to hand it off to the other man. The idea was that the tool was intercepting the polar energy, however briefly.

All that "everything has to be boy-girl-boy-girl" stuff is one of the things people now rail against, and not without reason. However, we can also see an advantage. Everyone is committed to generating and using a specific kind of energy, and every movement they make works in service of that energy. By the time you do magic or make an offering or meditate or whatever you've decided to do, there's no denying the buildup of power. The idea now is to take advantage of binary energy without being oppressive or exclusionary.

Section 2 is all about finding and using different polarities. Are there other energies that can be separated and brought together the way gender has been? This question may be the very essence of polarity work. Not every such polarity will work for every human, but there are many options. There's no harm in using energies that *aren't* universal if they work for *you*. If everyone in your group is heterosexual, you can work with exclusively heterosexual energy even though it would theoretically exclude queer people. You'd simply have to rethink if a queer person joined your group. If you kept your group closed to queer people in order to maintain your heterosexual polarity, *problematic* is the nicest word I could use to describe you, but I'm assuming good intentions here.

Let's talk about an energy already mentioned: erotic energy. While sexual arousal isn't a necessary or defining component of polarity, it's certainly a common one. Using this energy would exclude some (but not all) asexual people, but that leaves us with 99 percent of the population[23]—and it's just an example. The assumption here is also that there is a minimum

---

23. Wakefield, "This Is How Many LGBT People Identify as Asexual in America."

of two people, but solitary eroticism is also possible, and we'll talk about solitary polarity later on.

Two ways of leveraging erotic energy are *sublimation* and *contrast*. Contrast is the method at work in my original coven—the binary poles are kept in constant contrast. So, with erotic tension, you'd continually play on it throughout a ritual experience, perhaps with frequent pleasant touch, eye contact, and kissing. Everything done in ritual would be mildly erotic, building the energy bit by bit, interpolating whatever it is that will receive energy into the center of that contrast. Presumably the energy would ultimately be released by orgasm, either in or after the ritual.

In sublimation, you keep the poles apart as long as possible, building tension by refusing contact. A friend of mine met her girlfriend toward the beginning of the COVID pandemic (in a safe, socially distant context). When they decided they were ready to get physical, they each quarantined for ten days in order to be together safely. Imagine how *hot* that must have been, staying apart from anyone for that length of time for the sole purpose of being sexual at the end. Sublimation can be a damn sexy energy!

Generating energy via sublimation is also why a betrothed couple is kept apart, not even seeing each other, for some period of days prior to the wedding. The idea is that no matter how hard that electron tries to get to the proton, it's thwarted, so that when it's finally released, the energy generated is that much more explosive.

Twoness is relative. Something isn't on a pole unless there is another pole. Black isn't a pole unless there's white, but more to the point, *dark* isn't meaningful by itself. *Dark* is inherently *darker than*. The darkest gray contrasts as *light* when next to black. Dion Fortune said:

> Upon the subtle planes polarity is not fixed, but is relative; that which is more forceful than ourselves is positive towards us, and renders us negative towards itself....This fluidic, ever-fluctuating subtle polarity is one of the most important points in the practical workings.[24]

---

24. Fortune, *The Mystical Qabalah*, 124.

In any relationship, and in any polarity working, finding the twoness is an individual task. That is, we can use physical sex if we want to, as I was taught. Or we can find another contrast (such as we'll explore in sections 2 and 3).

My spouse and I identify as a butch/femme couple, and that means that even though we both have bodies identifiable as female, our gender expression is polar, and we both really enjoy and find power and beauty in that polarity, and work with it magically. Certainly, I've met people so much more feminine than me that I would be masculine by contrast, and the same is true about Professor Spouse and masculinity. These are relative traits—we have an individual polarity that works for us.

Gender expression is an example, though. As we explore polarities, we'll find the fluidity of polarity to be a recurring theme.

Adding a Third

Three is a magical number in so many ways, and when considered in the context of polarity, it is downright transformative. The existence of a third implies growth, change, evolution, a next generation, liminality, and, indeed, the existence of many.

Three as Creation

Heteronormative polarity holds the idea that the whole point of polarity magic is heterosexual reproduction. I'm a fan of heterosexual reproduction—most queer people I know, including me, came into the world that way. I even had a child of my own that way.

But people like metaphors they can relate to personally, and magic works best when that is true. The deepest parts of our mind, the subconscious and semiconscious and dreaming parts, from which great power can be drawn, need to relate, directly and viscerally, to the images we use. Thus, reproduction via heterosexual intercourse is not an ideal magical image for gay and lesbian people, or trans people, or infertile people, or people who choose not to reproduce.

Undoubtedly, creation, birth, and the emergence of new life *are* great images: *things being born.* In chapter 1 we saw that the creation of life needed a catalyst—an interaction. Polarity is that interaction, and from it, creation comes. In our little numerology game, one and two are the catalytic interaction and three is the creation. One and two are creators, while three is created. And yes, in the heterosexual reproduction model, one and two are mother and father and three is child. One and two, whether seen as "the God and the Goddess" or as Lynna Landstreet's active lightning strike and passive primordial sea, are the creative poles that lead to the three of Creation itself—humans, animals, plants, the whole thing. Even biblical creation is a process of separating pairs (night and day, firmament and waters) in order to create the world.

Naturally, in our deep minds, in magic, and in the occult, all creation is Creation. The original creation of life is the creation of every individual life. "As above, so below," the saying goes; "As the universe, so the soul." The macrocosm and the microcosm are one, and thus we see Creation in every creation, whether or not the polar energy is immediately apparent. So we see that creating a work of art is creation. Cooking dinner is creation. Every time something emerges from something substantively unlike what came before (babies are unlike adult humans, soup is unlike raw onions and chicken broth), it's creation.

Every act of creation is the interaction of some kind of force or energy (such as inspiration, motivation, passion, etc.) with some kind of form or shape (paint, canvas, raw ingredients). From this catalytic, polar interaction emerges something brand-new.

Third-as-creation is cyclical and eternal. Mythology is full not just of trinities but of tetrads (groups of four). This is because creation continues to the next generation.

For example, in Greek mythology, creation originates with the Titans. The "two" of Uranus and Gaia (Sky and Earth) brings forth children, including the "two" of Cronus and Rhea. Rhea gives birth to six Olympians, including the chief "two," Zeus and Hera. Cronus, Rhea, Zeus, and Hera were worshiped as a tetrad (among other things). Often, these mythological tetrads are incestuous—both Cronus and Rhea, and Zeus and Hera, are also siblings. So in a way, the four is also three: father, mother, and "offspring."

Giving birth to the third restarts the cycle of creation. Whether we like it or not, our parents tend to expect us to make them grandparents—they are looking for that cycle.

Every new creation has creative potential. Sometimes you sit down to write a five-hundred-word essay and the next thing you know you've written a book.

To be fair, not everything that is created becomes the "parent" pole in a new cycle of creation, just as not every human becomes a biological parent. The cycle of creativity may be internal to the creator—in which case, rebirth is present in *completion*. When you finish a creative endeavor, you make room in your life for more creation. When I'm focused on writing a book, it feels like the last book I'll ever write. I'm writing *this*. But when I hold the finished product in my hands, sometimes it's like a breeze blowing through me, and the next idea is born. Professor Spouse's creative outlet is in the kitchen, and over dinner, while enjoying her creative (and delicious) output, she'll sometimes say, "I could try this with sundried tomatoes…" The cycle begins again (yum).

Three is the completion of a polarity, but it's also the potential beginning of the next polarity. It's a stable resting spot, but also a new beginning. Magical indeed.

Three as Dialectics

I have been told that Hegel is the most difficult philosopher to understand, so I am definitely not going to try in any depth. I think we're safe in simply defining the process of *Hegelian dialectics* as it applies to our understanding of polarity and the third. It is:

A dialectic method of historical and philosophical progress that postulates (1) a beginning proposition called a thesis, (2) a negation of that thesis called the antithesis, and (3) a synthesis whereby the two conflicting ideas are reconciled to form a new proposition.

Although this method is commonly referred to as the Hegelian dialectic, Hegel actually attributed the terminology to Immanuel Kant.[25]

The way it works is this: There's a *thesis*: the original idea. Then the *antithesis* is proposed; it opposes or negates or argues against the thesis. Because both thesis and antithesis exist and can interact, *synthesis* is possible, meaning a brand-new idea that grows from its predecessors. The synthesis becomes the new thesis, and the process continues. Engels understood this as a philosophy of change, and Marx understood it as revolutionary.

It's not hard to see how dialectic progression relates to polarity. Thesis and synthesis can easily be seen as poles in a process; they create energy (synthesis) by their interaction. To me it's exciting to see that synthesis, the third, is continually being created by polar interaction. The synthesis becomes a new pole, and this creates an evolution of thought or energy. The process flows forward endlessly. Synthesis is possible only through the tension of seeming opposites working toward reconciliation.

Three as Liminality

A liminal state is a state between. It is the quality of standing on the border and being on neither side. Is twilight day or night? It is *liminal*; it is both/neither. It mediates the transition. When we talk about liminality, we recognize that a binary does exist, such as day and night, but that these two poles are not the full spectrum.

Queerness is often talked about as liminal, as mediating between genders. This is especially true in talking about Native American cultures, where *two-spirit* people are understood both as queer and as having a unique spiritual nature.[26] Queerness is liminal because it isn't *just* nonbinary; it stands between, mediates, and contains the binary, while also

---

25. Schnitker and Emmons, "Hegel's Thesis-Antithesis-Synthesis Model."

26. See, for example, Garry, "What It Really Means to Identify as Two-Spirit in Indigenous Culture," and Huard, "The Land Is Liminal."

(potentially) being outside the binary. Queerness takes the ingredients of male and female and makes soup.

Liminality makes itself known in systems that leverage polarity energy and seem very binary indeed. The tarot, for example, is an inheritor of a lot of Western magical thinking and is seen as very binary. Traditional tarot is gendered (although newer decks often consciously transcend that) and rooted in binary thinking. But look at the Lovers in the Waite-Smith tarot deck: they appear to be expressing a fairly straightforward polarity, but a nongendered angel hovers between them, holding a liminal space.

Everywhere that we see a binary (or a polarity), we can also see a liminal third helping us traverse the threshold. It's a fascinating thought exercise to take any polarity pair you can think of and ask yourself: What is the space between these two?

Three as a Mediating Space

Sometimes a third can be seen as a mediating space, holding the ground between polarities, easing tension where easing is needed. In alchemy, as we'll see in chapter 5, salt is the body that mediates between intellect/mercury and emotion/sulfur. Salt isn't liminal; it doesn't stand between sulfur and mercury the way twilight stands between night and day, or the way a crossroads stands between two roads. A mediating space is a third that is apart from the binary but also contributes a needed energy. The third can be a neutral ground, a demilitarized zone, or a ritual space where polarities can conjoin.

Three as Many

Why three? Why not four or five or fifty? It turns out that three contains all those other numbers. In *Third Sex, Third Gender*, we read:

> Why not four or five or myriad other categories of sex and gender? The presence of only two categories—the dyad—creates an inherent relationship of potential conflict....When, however, a third category or class is introduced, a new dynamic enters between the dyadic agents....The code of "thirdness" should not be taken literally to mean that in all times and places there are only three catego-

ries possible in human classification....The third is emblematic of other possible combinations that transcend dimorphism.[27]

In other words, three says "there aren't only two," but it doesn't necessarily bespeak an exact number when juxtaposed with a binary. In US politics, "third party" can mean the Greens, *or* the Independents, *or* the Socialist Workers Party, *or* the Libertarians. It can mean all of these at once. The word *third* here means many, perhaps infinite, options beyond the binary.

Seeing this, we can understand that one of the powers of threeness is how it takes us from black and white to the rainbow.

One: Wholeness

In two, we find the energy of polarity, a source of immense power and often wisdom. In two, we also find the oppressiveness of the binary. In three, we find creation, synthesis, and a rainbow of possibilities. In the end, though, almost everyone who has ever touched upon polarity comes back to one.

We've already seen this in chapter 1 in the yin/yang symbol: the circle containing the symbol is oneness, and wholeness, and is intended to show us an underlying truth. We'll visit oneness again in alchemy. One of the most important alchemists in history was Miriam the Jewess, also known as Mary or Maria the Jewess or Maria the Prophetess. The alchemical *Axiom of Maria* states:

> One becomes two, two becomes three,
> and by means of the third and fourth
> achieves unity; thus two are but one.
> Invert nature and you will find that what you seek.
> Join the male and the female, and you will find what is sought.
> —Miriam the Jewess, 300 CE[28]

---

27. Herdt, *Third Sex, Third Gender: Beyond Sexual Dimorphism in Culture and History*, 19–20.
28. Patai, *The Jewish Alchemists*, 66.

Alchemy is a dense and complex subject, one we'll revisit in enough detail for it to make a bit more sense. Here we get a taste—the alchemist divides male from female for the purpose of reuniting them at a higher level, because they are ultimately one. In alchemy, separation and division are steps taken in order to achieve the exaltation of coming back together. "What is sought" is oneness.

In the Kabbalah (another subject we'll get back to), everything is based on oneness, and everything is also seen as a polarity. The Tree of Life is divided into ten *sephirot* (spheres), each of which exists on one of three pillars. The spheres are gendered, the pillars are gendered, and the energies exist in a constant interplay of poles. But the sephirot are also known as *emanations*—they emanate from *Ain Soph*, the Endless One. It is true that Kabbalah is Jewish mysticism, and therefore rooted in monotheism, while most p-word folks are decidedly not monotheistic. But the point is not that the "one" here is "the One God"; the point is that the polar energies of the Tree of Life cannot be properly understood except in the context of knowing them as ultimately one.

I find special delight in uncovering talk about oneness, about transcending polarity, and even about transcending gender in occult writings from the Victorian and Edwardian eras. It tickles me that the material that has often been most oppressive in its execution actually contains a genuinely diverse and nonbinary understanding—if only its own authors could perceive the meaning of their own words. For instance, in Dion Fortune's *The Sea Priestess* we read, "But the ancients…said that the soul was bisexual."[29]

Magical and spiritual literature is full of quotes like that, side by side with gender-essentialist quotes telling us the opposite, as if they didn't realize what they were saying. Occultists from as early as the nineteenth and early twentieth centuries tell us that men are *this* and women are *that*, and that's just the way the energy *is*. Their material is always overflowing with quotes belying it, as if the authors somehow subconsciously knew that the binary is not quite as binary as they believed.

---

29. Fortune, *The Sea Priestess*, 177. Here, *bisexual* means "having two sexes" and is not about attraction or orientation.

In various magical systems, we find the idea of polarity as a circuit completed within oneself. A typical teaching goes like this: Each individual finds the "male" and "female" within themselves and creates an energy circuit. For example, occultist Charles Seymour suggested in his magical diaries that the act of working with a magical partner was for those not yet adept enough to complete the circuit internally: "The idea of the adept as a self-polarizing entity was…constant to his [Seymour's] conception of magic's aim….He deliberately sought this unity with the help of another soul in a different sex."[30]

This type of teaching is also found in several Wiccan traditions. Because traditional Wicca has stressed gender polarity and has sometimes been oppressive about it, this concept of the "inner circuit" has allowed people to work within traditional Wicca in a way they find recognizable—keeping the structure of a polarity-based system while simultaneously overcoming its strictures. Self-polarity, like self-eroticism, is a legitimate experience. It can be harder to reach the heights of power in that context, but it can work well.

But this circuit is not just a convenient substitute for heteronormativity. It's actually saying something deep, and something quite ancient, about polarity: It's an energy that occurs in a larger whole, and the whole, the One, must always be kept in mind. That is, if we think of the poles only as themselves, we're missing a lot of the magic.

Journal/Discussion Prompts

- Were you taught any polarity customs or rules in regard to how to conduct ritual? Are they meaningful to you? Did they use sublimation or contrast?
- Think of anything you have created. Can you identify the polar forces that preceded it?
- Think of any polarity or binary pair. Can you identify the liminal space between the poles?

---

30. Richardson, *20th Century Magic and the Old Religion*, 72.

- Look around the room you are in now. Do you see any polarities? Begin with yourself—body and mind are often thought of as a polarity, and there are probably many others. For each, can you identify the third? Can you identify wholeness?

Chapter Three

Polarity and Sexuality

Now that we've defined some complicated terms related to sex and sexuality, we can circle back to the subject of sexuality and polarity. Why do people think that polarity is sex, and why isn't it? What is the role of sexuality and romance in polarity magic?

The *Hieros Gamos*

Hieros gamos ("sacred marriage") is a ritualized sexual union of a goddess and a god. This can be enacted sexually or symbolically or not enacted at all. Perhaps a story is recited instead. Variations are found throughout the ancient world, and some still exist. In Catholicism, the Paschal candle is plunged three times into the baptismal font. This candle is thought by many to be a sexual symbol of Christ, the groom, impregnating the Church, his bride. In the Western Mystery Traditions, there are many examples of such ritual acts.

The culture of Sumer, four thousand years old, brings us the oldest known human literature, and in it we find a record of the sacred marriage of the goddess Inanna to the shepherd Dumuzi. The marriage rite was enacted by the priestess of the goddess and the king.[31] The surviving poetry is explicitly sexual and replete with agricultural double entendres,

---

31. Wolkstein and Kramer, *Inanna, Queen of Heaven and Earth*, 124.

such as "My lord Dumuzi is ready for the holy loins. / The plants and herbs in his field are ripe."[32] The poetry itself also contains ritual instructions.[33]

Here, as in ancient Greece, Ireland, and elsewhere, we find sacred marriage ensuring the fertility of the land, including crops, animals, and human beings. In ancient Ireland, the sacred marriage conferred sovereignty.[34] The king had the right to rule because he had fertilized/been joined with the land itself in the body of the goddess. This distinction between fertility and sovereignty is kind of moot. If the land is not fertile, if people starve, then the king is considered illegitimate. So whether the point of the ritual was to confer kingship or to plow Inanna's field, the result was the same.

The Great Rite of Wicca

In Wicca, the ritual of the Great Rite exemplifies the way that polarity and sex are seen to interconnect. It can be considered a modern *hieros gamos*. There are other examples in modern p-word practices, but Wicca is the one I know best, and so is the example I'll use.

The Great Rite actually refers to two different ritual acts. They are known as the "token" or "symbolic" Great Rite and the "true" Great Rite. The true Great Rite is a sacred ritual that includes heterosexual intercourse (or sometimes other kinds of sex) as its culmination. In the token Great Rite, ritual tools are used in a manner that is suggestive of intercourse: an athame (witch's knife), considered "male," is plunged into a cup of wine, considered "female." Typical language used in such a ritual might be "As the athame is to the male, so the cup is to the female; and conjoined, they become one in truth."[35] (Some people substitute the wand for the athame.)

The Great Rite appears to be derived from Aleister Crowley's Gnostic Mass,[36] which contains a similar ritual, called the *mystic marriage*, wherein

---

32. Wolkstein and Kramer, *Inanna, Queen of Heaven and Earth*, 41.

33. Wolkstein and Kramer, *Inanna, Queen of Heaven and Earth*, 107–10.

34. Fradenburg, *Women & Sovereignty.*

35. Janet and Stewart Farrar, *A Witches' Bible: Eight Sabbats for Witches*, 46.

36. Crowley, *Annotated Liber XV (Book 15) O.T.O.*

the priest, having invoked and adored the priestess with passionate language, plunges his lance into the cup of wine.

The Great Rite presents the problem of all such workings: What does it mean, and how gender essentialist is it? Is it a polarity working? Is it sex? It's unclear.

It's not true to say the Great Rite is inherently exclusive of queerness. It may have been thought of as completely heterosexual in the past, but Wicca is changing with the times. Jason Mankey writes, "Because many people perceive [the Great Rite] as an exclusively heteronormative practice (an idea that I and many other Witches disagree with), there are some Witches and covens who want nothing to do with it."[37] Once we say that though, we have to figure out what it *is* that is not heteronormative.

Love, Lust, and Fertility

Assuming that everyone is heterosexual and gender normative means that you can enact a ceremony like the Great Rite without examining it closely. In any magical sexual ritual performed by a heterosexual couple, there can be multiple dimensions worked simultaneously. For queer people to access the same power, we have to take the ritual apart and look at its components, and determine how much of it is gender essentialist or heterosexual, or not either of those things. We don't have the privilege of having it all exist in an undifferentiated sexy stew.

In my book *The Elements of Ritual*, I say:

> The union of the cup and athame represents the union of the Goddess and the God. There are several different meanings that Wiccans will ascribe to this union: that it represents **procreation,** that it represents **love,** or that it represents the **union of opposites.**[38]

Sexual rites can also be a recognition, enactment, or celebration of fertility. As a heterosexual rite, it can be a form of imitative magic: you imitate the thing you want to magically bring about. Even a nonfertile opposite-sex

---

37. Mankey, *Transformative Witchcraft*, 317.

38. Lipp, *The Elements of Ritual*, 188.

couple can have their act of intercourse be symbolic of a core act of fertile creation. "This is how reproduction happens" is a magically potent way of creating magical reproduction of whatever kind is sought. For this component of sexual rites, queer people might be excluded, and could choose a different, nonsexual way of symbolizing fertility, or they might use penetrative sex to symbolize fertility (just as nonfertile heterosexual couples do).

Considering a sexual rite equivalent to a fertility rite can be particularly true for Wicca, which has frequently been described, especially a few decades ago, as a "fertility religion." If symbolizing fertility is the intention of a sexual or sexually symbolic rite, you could fairly argue that it should be done heterosexually, to represent procreation (although you could also argue that a queer couple is as capable of symbolizing fertility as a nonfertile heterosexual couple).

While it's possible for a queer couple to enact heterosexual fertility, that's not necessarily a great fit and not necessarily comfortable for the queer couple. On the other hand, the book *Casting a Queer Circle* points out that there are a lot of examples of plant and animal procreation in nature that aren't heteronormative at all, and includes a delightful and playful fertility ritual that mimics snail reproduction.[39]

Ironically, many homophobes will say that queer people can't do this or that sort of magic (such as the Great Rite) because they're not fertile, but when they dig into a discussion of what the Great Rite really means, the emphasis is almost always on love and almost never on fertility. (This is not unlike the arguments against same-sex marriage, which had to twist into knots to explain that same-sex couples couldn't marry because they were infertile, but it was *perfectly fine* for infertile opposite-sex couples to marry because that's not the point of marriage anyway. Whatever.)

Which brings us to love. In *The Elements of Ritual*, I point out that fertility can be present when love is absent (and vice versa).[40] As thinking about misogyny and consent came more and more to influence modern Pagan

---

39. Minai, *Casting a Queer Circle*, 93–94.

40. Lipp, *The Elements of Ritual*, 190.

and Wiccan rituals, the idea of venerating fertility without a consent component started to seem a little icky. That's where love—already venerated in such religions—comes in.

Where sexual rites and sex magic are involved, love can be powerful, and deep, and can also be a little prudish. The Farrars say, *"Sex magic as such should only be worked by a couple for whom intercourse*[41] *is a normal part of their relationship."*[42] (Italics in the original—they were really emphasizing the point!) They're talking about a few different things at once. You can definitely read between the lines that they mean something like, it's not okay to have sex without love, *especially* not if the sex is magical. We can set that aside. They're primarily saying that the power of a sexual rite is so intense that it can alter the relationship of the people performing it, and this isn't necessarily a good idea for people who aren't even used to having sex together. Most of us know that a relationship changes once sex comes into the picture; a relationship changes *again* when sex magic is introduced. Introducing the sex magic before the sex is weird and not good for the future of the relationship. (The Farrars were much more dogmatic than that, but you get the point.)

The Farrars are also talking about a loving relationship as being a core part of sexual ritual. Mankey says, "In its simplest form, the Great Rite is a celebration of union,"[43] and then goes on to offer a lovely kind of Great Rite that is completely nonsexual and focuses on breath connection.[44]

Obviously, love as a ground for a rite that has been previously seen as heterosexual is wide open for queerness, including queer orientations, gender queerness, and asexuality. Anyone can love another human deeply, though not necessarily romantically. Sexual rituals structured around the

---

41. A lot of older authors conflate sex magic with intercourse. You definitely can do sex magic in every way you have sex, and intercourse is not a part of that for everyone, despite what the Farrars say here.

42. Janet and Stewart Farrar, *A Witches' Bible: The Witches' Way*, 171.

43. Mankey, *Transformative Witchcraft*, 294.

44. Mankey, *Transformative Witchcraft*, 325–27, "Soul to Soul: A Rite for Connection."

energy of love and/or romance are easily queered. There's no need to hang gender on them at all.

Sexual rites and sex magic can also be the magic of lust and passion. (I didn't include this angle in *The Elements of Ritual*.) Not everyone is comfortable separating love and sex, but the fact is they *are* separate. It's special and wonderful when they coincide. But that wonderfulness is often used to denigrate lust for lust's sake. The wild and wanton sexuality of goddesses such as Aphrodite and Ishtar is something to celebrate. When passionate feelings run wild within us, that can truly be godlike and magical. Sex is one way in which humans are able to transcend separateness and experience something like oneness, and this can happen even when romance isn't involved. Obviously, consent needs to be a part of this, as well as moral integrity—lying in order to have a lustful experience is *not good*.

Each of these components of a sexual (or symbolically sexual) ritual can be rooted in polarity. A loving connection can be unity or it can be a blending of differences into a magical third. Sexual passion also has a polar nature: the desire of one for the other is a rush toward completing a circuit. And fertility is polar, sperm rushing toward egg, again creating the magical third.

Finally, the whole point of a sexual rite can be polarity: the "union of opposites."

Invocation

Both ancient and modern rites suggest that an invocation of the deities into the bodies of those enacting ritual *hieros gamos* has occurred. This is explicit, for example, in the Gnostic Mass. The idea is that of transcendence: it is not the priestess who is having this sex; it is the goddess herself.

Invocation like this is common in modern Wicca and is known as *drawing down the moon*. (The phrase *drawing down the sun* is often used for a man, and these phrases tend to be used whether or not the deities being invoked are lunar or solar.) Invocation is common in ceremonial magic as well. Variations occur in many religions, not just in sexual rites. For example, it is used to attain oracular vision in modern Heathenry, or just to be in the presence of the deity, as in some Hindu rites.

Since it "isn't really the person," some people think that a preexisting love or sexual relationship between those performing a sacred marriage rite isn't necessary. However, the existence of a symbolic version of the ritual (such as the lance in the cup) would seem to belie this. People are people; they like agency over what happens to their bodies. Some invocatory trance results in the ego-self's loss of consciousness; that is, some people don't remember anything that happened to them while their body housed a deity—but some people do. It seems to depend as much on the individual as on the specific religion and ritual technique.

Kabbalistic Sacred Marriage

We'll talk more about Kabbalah in chapter 5 when we get into the magical and philosophical sources of our modern concept of polarity. For now, let's take a peek at the way sacred marriage manifests in Kabbalah. (I'll be speaking about traditional Jewish Kabbalah going back to the thirteenth century, long before the Hermetic Qabala familiar to many occultists.)

Remember that the Kabbalistic Tree of Life is composed of ten sephirot (spheres), which are ultimately emanations of the One God. In much of Kabbalah though, God is described in almost polytheistic terms. God's kingship (seen as *Tiferet*, the sixth sephirah—a *sephirah* is a single sphere) and his presence on earth (*Malkut* or *Shekhinah*, the tenth sephirah) are described as a god and goddess. Passionate sexual imagery of the union of the King (Tiferet) and His Bride (the Shekhinah) is found throughout the *Zohar*, the most significant text of Kabbalah. There's extensive discussion of how, during the time of the Temple in Jerusalem, the King and his Shekhinah were united on their marriage bed in the Temple, but since the destruction of the second Temple in 70 CE, the Shekhinah has been exiled from her King. The *Zohar* is florid in its description of their ancient sexual pleasure, and equally passionate about the sorrow of their separation.

Sexual love between a pious husband and wife is considered a way to help God and Shekhinah reunite in the marriage bed. To quote *The Hebrew*

Goddess, probably the seminal work on the subject of God's relationship with his Bride in Judaism:

> The union between man and wife was considered by the Zohar a replica of the union between God and the Shekhina, and, at the same time, the fulfillment of one of the greatest sacred commandments, because it mystically promoted that divine union and thus contributed to the oneness and wholeness of the deity.[45]

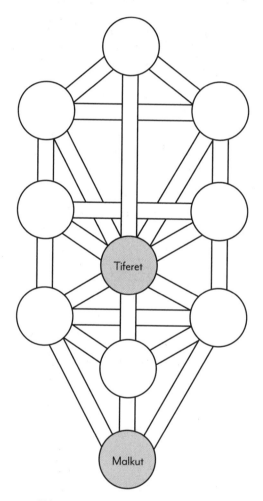

Tiferet and Malkut on the Tree of Life

---

45. Patai, *The Hebrew Goddess,* 162.

In thinking about the spiritual power of this sex act, we can know that even though this is any ordinary couple, not a priestess and king, and the act is not surrounded by ritual, the sacred meaning of it is clearly of a piece with what we've learned of other forms of *hieros gamos*. This particular sexual ritual has as its sole purpose the union of God with his Beloved; there isn't a fertility or sovereignty component, as found in other such rites. Yet like other *hieros gamos* rituals, it is a deeply reverent enactment, through human sexuality, of the presence of deity.

Indeed, the great Kabbalistic sage Isaac Luria believed that unification of God with his Shekhinah was the purpose of Jewish prayer, healing the rift in the world. "The holy marriage of Tiferet and Shekhinah is the most important task that the mystic assumes in his quest."[46]

The Hebrew song "Lecha Dodi" ("Come My Beloved") is a Kabbalistic song, ostensibly a greeting to the Sabbath Bride, with veiled meaning about the reunion of Tiferet and Shekhinah.[47] The song was written in the sixteenth century by Shlomo ben Moshe Halevi Alqabetz, "with liberal borrowings from earlier versions."[48]

In the sixteenth century, (male) Kabbalists would process out to the fields (referred to as the "sacred apple orchard") on Friday night and ecstatically sing "Lecha Dodi" or another song to the bride, and then

> return home to be received by their wives—the wife in this instance became for the husband the earthly representative of the Shekhina, with whom he was about to perform that night the sacred act of cohabitation in imitation of, and in mystical sympathy with, the supernal union between God the King and His wife.[49]

This sexual union was surrounded by ritual similar to that of a wedding.

46. Ariel, *The Mystic Quest*, 97.

47. Ariel, *The Mystic Quest*, 105–9.

48. Patai, *The Hebrew Goddess*, 268.

49. Patai, *The Hebrew Goddess*, 272.

Other versions of greeting the Sabbath bride see the marriage as with
Yesod, with *Yesod* being used as a euphemism for the penis.[50]

"Lecha Dodi" remains a popular song to sing in synagogues during Friday night Kabbalat Shabbat services to this day, albeit without the sexual
rite.

Sex Magic

Sex magic is any act of magic that uses sex to fuel the work. A lot of writers
about sex magic want to obfuscate that, talking about "the techniques" of
sex magic as if there were a finite number of correct ones.

The fact is, magic involves sending power to an intended target for
some specified purpose. That power has to come from somewhere. There
are quite a number of ways to generate power,[51] and one of them is sex.
In many ways, it is not that different from raising power by drumming and
dancing.

The history of Western ceremonial sex magic practices can be traced
from Tantra in India to Sufi mystics in the Middle East to the Knights Templar.[52] It was famously practiced by notorious magician Aleister Crowley
(which is why the press dubbed him the "wickedest man in the world").

When polarity is seen as *the* way to do sex magic, that sex is often seen
as having a heterosexual couple as the participants, but it ain't necessarily
so. Sex magic can be performed alone, in a couple, or using group sex.
There are couples' techniques relying heavily on simultaneous orgasm, and
others where all of the energy is channeled through one partner's orgasm.

We'll talk more about sex magic in section 3.

Polarity in Sexual Rites and Sexual Magic

In each of the instances of sexual magic or sexual ritual described above,
the energy generated may or may not depend on polarity.

---

50. Patai, *The Hebrew Goddess*, 273.

51. Lipp, *Magical Power for Beginners*, 86.

52. Kraig, *Modern Sex Magick*, 4.

In the ancient examples of *hieros gamos* ritual, we find the polarity magic of fertility and lust, but not love. The priestess and priest or king performing the rite don't have to know or like or connect to each other. The gods are acting *through* them.

We can assume that a fertility rite always has polarity. Just as a light bulb can intercept the energy rushing from electron to proton, so can a womb intercept the energy of sperm rushing to egg. The circuit is completed by conception.

In the example of the Great Rite, we saw that love and lust might or might not be polar but could be queer with or without polarity. We also saw that the rite could explicitly represent polarity itself, without an intermediary.

The Kabbalistic sacred marriage is almost always seen as polar. The Tree of Life is elaborately gendered. However, when we dig more deeply into Kabbalah, we'll find some remarkable subtleties to that.

For now, though, we can see that almost every kind of sexual magic or sexual ritual can include polarity, but maybe not in the way we've assumed, and definitely in many ways that can be inclusive of queerness.

Chapter Four

Where Polarity Stands Today

Now that we understand what polarity is and is not, let's look at its current status in the various p-word communities. Next we'll dig into the history of these ideas.

The occult community I grew up in has changed rapidly, as the world has changed. The gender essentialism and occasional homophobia in the books I read early on was often invisible to me because it was so commonplace. Trans and nonbinary people didn't even exist in such books. Our culture, broadly, has become more willing to recognize queer people as fully human and has begun to notice that not everyone's gender lives on a binary. None of this was true in 1981 when I first started studying the occult. None of it was true even into the 1990s and early 2000s. Books I loved and recommended back then now appear to me to be hopelessly dated and sometimes oppressive. Recognizing the rapid change of society, and of the occult part of society, has been complex for many older practitioners, even queer ones like me. (Some older practitioners, including queer ones, have refused to make the effort and have fallen flat on their faces as a result. I'm hoping to avoid that.)

It's certainly not easy to step forward into the present moment with a clear vision of exactly how much is relegated to the past and how much is happening now. It's not easy to have a finger on the pulse of "the magical community today." It's a huge and growing community, with a great deal of diversity. Various types of practitioners sometimes have no interaction with other types and may not even be aware they exist. The magical world is in person, it's online, it's in print. It occurs at large, medium, and small public gatherings and in private, often secretive groups. It proliferates on a wide variety of social media platforms, not all of which I'm on top of. To improve my understanding, I've looked in all of these places, but we're all in bubbles to a certain extent. You, in your bubble, may experience a p-word community utterly different from my own.

That said, I see some basic trends and prominent ideas about polarity and its place in the occult. I will attempt to describe those ideas and trends next.

Polarity Is What It Always Was

By this I mean there's a broad segment of the magical world that continues to understand polarity as it was taught to me in the 1980s: polarity is essential, it is gender normative, and that's it on that.

There are many Pagan, Heathen, and magical groups that may or may not even use polarity as a concept that are content to exist in the world as if there were no queer people in it. There are groups that talk about the importance of valuing women's voices and agency and embracing feminism, for example, but with no language whatsoever that indicates that some of these women will never be wives to men or want to be. There are websites and blogs that talk about modernizing the values of what it means to be a man without acknowledging that some men are queer.

I have a book about polarity magic (published in the twenty-first century) on my desk right now that has no entries in its index for any queer-related words. It is 100 percent about the relationship between male and female, and it doesn't even define those terms, assuming that everyone already knows the definitions.

Sometimes you find that groups/books/websites/social media pages will talk about how queer people may or may not fit into their polarity system. This is sometimes a veneer of inclusivity that asks LGBTQIA+

people to, essentially, behave. This quote from Janet and Stewart Farrar is infamous: "We have even had one or two homosexual members during our coven's history, when they have been prepared and able to assume the role of their actual gender while in a Wiccan context."[53] This book was published in 1984, and we all know that attitudes have changed a lot since then. I don't know what Stewart's thoughts on this were at the time of his death in 2000. Janet has published very little in the past twenty years, and nothing on the subject of gender or sexuality. I am not judging either of them based on something they wrote so long ago.

The fact is, though, that this 1984 quote is assumed by a lot of people to be representative of Wicca in general today. In some corners of the magical world, the quote represents an attitude—and even a set of rules—that still exists, an attitude that is patronizing, ignorant, and harmful.

The controversy that blew up around PantheaCon, once the largest annual occult gathering in North America, back in 2011 and 2012 is fairly well known.[54] In 2011 a ritual that had been announced as for "all women" excluded trans women. After enormous controversy and conflict, the same ritual returned a year later, this time announced as for "genetic women only." Protests were scheduled to occur at the same time as the ritual.

Another example is a recent controversy within the U.S. Grand Lodge of the O.T.O., in which a policy intended to be inclusive of trans people inherently excluded nonbinary people, saying people could choose to be a Priestess or a Priest but not both.[55]

The Wiccan example in the quote from the Farrars is explicitly about polarity, while the examples from PantheaCon and the O.T.O. are about gender more generally. Yet it's pretty clear that they all are about defining a status quo in a magical context.

I could continue to offer a string of quotes and stories from a variety of magic/magick streams, but they're probably no fun to read.

---

53. Janet and Stewart Farrar, *The Witches' Way*, 170.

54. Pitzl-Waters, "Gender, Transgender, Politics, and Our Beloved Community."

55. Gordon, "Gender Is Not a Zero-Sum Game."

There are many groups today that will not accept trans members, or will do so only under narrow conditions, and some that won't accept any queer members at all; and, as in the example of the O.T.O., there are groups that accept "men" and "women," including fully understanding that trans women are women and trans men are men, but that will not accept nonbinary, agender, or other gender-diverse people. In addition to groups that just pretend there's no queerness or those that are pretend-inclusive, there are of course groups out there that are frankly and bluntly homophobic and transphobic. These cases are sometimes the policy of an individual group (a single coven or lodge or what have you) or of a tradition as a whole.

More broadly, setting aside specific issues of inclusivity, gender norma-tivity prevails in many people's magical view of polarity. In many schools of thought, the world is still divided into poles assigned to gender, so that passive is female and active is male, receptive is female and projective is male, and so on. In Wicca, this may be described duotheistically, as "the Lord" and "the Lady," with each having half of the characteristics of a dualistic reality. The individual polarities (such as passive / active) have great power, but assigning them to gendered headings is problematic at the least.

For one thing, we should notice how incredibly culture-bound such polarities are. In the West, we tend to assign compassion and kindness to the female and strictness and discipline to the male. Mothers are Good Cop and fathers are Bad Cop: "Just wait 'til your father gets home!" But in the mythology of the Middle East, we find gentle, peaceable fathers and "chastising," fierce mothers.[56] This carries over into the Kabbalah, where the Pillar of Mercy is considered male and the Pillar of Severity is consid-ered female. It is remarkable how many Western occultists incorporate Kabbalah into a dualistic system that otherwise has "feminine" as soft and "masculine" as hard, and never seem to notice the contradiction. (Natu-rally, this isn't the only polarity where a culture-bound definition of gender is meaningful.)

---

56. Patai, *The Hebrew Goddess*, 78–79.

Polarity Should Be Ignored or Isn't a Thing

Social media is overrun with the "revelation" that polarity is a load of crap, as well as definitions of Wicca that simply omit the concept entirely. Younger Wiccans are often ignorant of Wicca's origins in the Western Mystery Traditions and its ties to the Golden Dawn in particular, so they may not realize that some concept of polarity is built into Wicca's DNA.

That said, there is no problem with looking at polarity and deciding it doesn't belong in your system. In addition, there are definitely parts of the magical world in which working with polarity is not, and never has been, a part of the paradigm. Druidry, for example, doesn't work with polarity as an energetic concept. The Feri Tradition may be the oldest tradition of modern witchcraft that doesn't work with polarity energy.[57] In Minoan Wicca, polarity is considered an entirely internal circuit and isn't worked with a partner, as is done in most magical traditions.

In her book *Outside the Charmed Circle,* Misha Magdalene writes about polarity from the point of view of an initiate of both Feri (no polarity, really) and Gardnerian Wicca (lots of it).[58] Ultimately, she boils it down to a discussion of harmful gender essentialism, homophobia, transphobia, and misogyny in Wicca. She explicitly does *not* reject polarity:

> I'm not here to abolish gender or polarity. I realize this will surprise some folks (and disappoint others), but I won't presume to deny someone's identity or lived experience, even those folks whose identities and experiences are alien to me.[59]

Reading the book, I got an impression that Magdalene was rejecting polarity, so I'm glad to have had a conversation with her later on in which she pointed out the above quote. Nonetheless, because so much homophobic, transphobic, and anti-queer baggage accompanies polarity, she explicitly

---

57. Walker, "Feri FAQ."

58. Magdalene, *Outside the Charmed Circle,* 96–113.

59. Magdalene, *Outside the Charmed Circle,* 113.

chooses not to include it as a subject matter in her writing. As a result, the magic she presents in print omits polarity as an energy.

Other magical writers insist that polarity isn't needed. For example, in their article "Polarity in Sex Magick," Ellwood and Lupa write:

> We feel polarity is an unnecessary approach to sex in general, that has caused far more harm and misunderstanding precisely because it is cultural, as opposed to biological.
>
> Yet, incorporation of polarity occurs all too often even in modern texts.[60]

For these magicians, polarity isn't necessary. I agree, but I also find it powerful, and I find my magical work enhanced by its presence.

New Conceptions of Polarity

A lot of magical people are doing amazing work in uncovering new ways to express and define magical polarity. For example, in the article "Understanding Polarity in the 21st Century," Over Alder writes:

> Polarity is, in essence, a constant interaction between more than one force or element. It is the movement, the striving of those forces, and the rhythm in it, that creates the dynamism. As occultists, witches or magicians we observe the underlying patterns of that rhythm, get insights and tap into it, or try to emulate it—either conscious or unconsciously.
>
> Therefore, new possibilities mean new insights. Why Love—Hate? And not Love—Death (Thanatos & Eros), or Love—Soul (Eros & Psyche).[61]

Good stuff!

In his essay on polarity in the book *Queer Magic*, Ivo Dominguez, Jr. writes, "The polarities we can experience are relative rather than absolute. Relative polarities are non-binary as a direct consequence of the mixed

---

60. Ellwood and Lupa, "Polarity in Sex Magick."

61. Alder, "Understanding Polarity in the 21st Century."

nature of the world in which we live."[62] He then goes on to explore the value of keeping the magical teaching about polarity as a jumping-off point, and then explores it on a physical and metaphysical level.

The book *Casting a Queer Circle* is focused on inclusivity of queer people and queer concerns, seeing "binary polarity" as "one dynamic amongst many."[63] Author Thista Minai returns to polarity in the section on raising energy, noting:

> The power of polarity lies in embracing how opposites enhance and highlight one another. Tension, separation, and union between polar opposites all create surges of energy that can power ritual and magic....
>
> There are many other types of polarity [than gender] to work with in magic...There are many ways in which we complement each other in our differences. Working with dynamic polarity in circle means focusing on those differences and using the interplay between them to generate energy.[64]

Minai then goes on to discuss synergy and solidarity as other forms of energetic interplay between people.

There are some ideas about polarity, though, that seem to me simply like an effort to minimize its significance within the context of a tradition that requires it. For example, *Transformative Witchcraft* (a generally excellent book) defines polarity broadly as "a union of at least two forces,"[65] and then adds that masturbation is polarity because it's the union of friction with genitalia. To me, that's too loose a definition—polarity isn't *any* two forces, but is the energy created by their striving toward each other. I'm not persuaded that friction alone meets the definition.

In an article titled "Polarity, Gender, and Fertility," Yvonne Aburrow has a clear, modern, and helpful set of polarities: "Other ways of looking

---

62. Harrington and Kulystin, *Queer Magic*, 175–78.

63. Minai, *Casting a Queer Circle*, 9.

64. Minai, *Casting a Queer Circle*, 111–12.

65. Mankey, *Transformative Witchcraft*, 296.

at polarity could include self and other, lover and beloved, spirit and matter, energy and form, and so on."[66] However, in the same article, Aburrow defines polarity similarly to Mankey, as virtually any tension or difference:

> Some Wiccans take the view that polarity can only be created by the interaction of a male body and a female body.
>
> This is definitely not true, as I have demonstrated in several workshops by getting people to make magic with the tension of opposites such as extrovert and introvert, morning people and evening people, beer lovers and wine lovers, and many other polarities. I generally do this in workshops just to demonstrate that it is possible to create polarity using any difference; I don't do it in every ritual. It is worth doing as a magical exercise to prove to yourself that polarity can be made with any pair of opposites—we have even done it with people who like Marmite and people who like chocolate.[67]

Setting aside the difficulty you'd find in the US coming up with *anyone* who likes marmite, not all of these tensions are polarities, and some are not even opposites (wine and beer?). What Aburrow is demonstrating in ritual is that *energy* can be created by tension, but they aren't teasing out *polarity* energy. There is no distinction made here between the polarity that exists, for example, between introvert and extrovert energies and the simple, nonpolar difference between choices in alcoholic beverages.

What's clear is that the use of polarity, and how it is understood, is profoundly in flux at the moment. Parts of the p-word community are throwing out polarity entirely, parts are working (successfully and less so) to create new definitions, and parts are holding the line at an older concept, using outmoded definitions of gender to enforce that concept. In the next chapter, we'll explore what those "older" concepts really are. How old are

---

66. Aburrow, "Polarity, Gender, and Fertility."

67. Aburrow, "Polarity, Gender, and Fertility."

they? Where did they come from? What can they teach us about polarity and about our magic generally?

The Personal Is the Magical

In second-wave feminism, "The personal is the political" was a rallying cry. (The source of this is unknown; it is most identified with an essay by that name by Carol Hanisch, but Hanisch didn't come up with the phrase.)

The idea of the personal being political (and vice versa) is that the small things that make up an individual life are not different from political concerns. Today we understand that, for example, childcare is a meaningful political issue, but in the early 1970s child care was "merely personal" and not worthy of serious political consideration. Identifying personal concerns as political concerns meant women's lives mattered.

I'm stealing the phrase to say that the personal is the magical. It's not enough to study and learn a magical or spiritual system and follow its rules. It has to be personal. The personal lives of the practitioners of magic have to inform the systems we use, and the systems have to recognize that the impact of its practitioners is meaningful and valuable.

In the early 1990s, a dear friend of mine was dying of AIDS. He said that people he knew, people with New Age beliefs, kept telling him he'd created his own illness. This infuriated me. If you create your own reality, then can't you choose a paradigm within that reality that includes *kindness*? Can't compassion figure into the equation? Creating your own reality cannot and must not be an excuse to be dismissive of the suffering of others.

I see this lack of compassion all over the place in discussions of Wiccan traditions and magical systems. The idea is that the system itself is transpersonal and that no individual has the right to have an impact on it.

So, sure, some people walk into a tradition or system with the idea of smashing it, or at least with an excess of hubris about how things are going to go. Traditional Wicca asks humility of the seeker. We don't look kindly upon newcomers approaching our traditions with "How will you adapt and change to suit me?" being the first question on their lips. It is, frankly, annoying.

So, for example, when someone comes to me and says that they have a very demanding, busy life, and the study system I offer for training in Wicca is too much for them to handle, to me they are saying this isn't a good time in their life for in-depth study. That's okay; they can visit rituals without an expectation that they take on the study system. But if they're saying "and therefore the system should be made less demanding," that doesn't fly. Professor Spouse gets this in her professional life with her college students; they need to pass and they don't study, therefore she should pass them despite their incomplete work. Alas, that's not how the world works.

On the other hand, there are far too many magical systems, groups, covens, groves, and the like that treat every request for inclusion as though it's coming from a spoiled brat who is asking for grade inflation. In fact, the request for inclusion comes from human beings, by virtue of their humanness. Not everyone can be included everywhere. For example, poor rhythm makes you an unavoidably bad match for a drumming group. But being inclusive of humans as they are, embracing their humanity, and showing kindness and creativity toward apparent conflicts is the least that any of us can do. Maybe you can't drum with no rhythm—would you like to be in charge of setting up the chairs?

Queerness

In issues of queerness, creativity and inclusivity can take center stage. Where a group or system is working with a rigid definition of gender and/or gender polarity, an increasingly visible subsection of people just don't fit that definition. Inclusivity means making an effort to have room for differences you hadn't previously considered. Creativity means discovering or inventing new ways to make that happen.

Too often the response is "Oh well, too bad for you. Find a different group." Rejecting someone's lack of musical ability, or their unwillingness or unavailability to do the amount of work a group requires, is one thing. Rejecting someone's core identity, it seems to me, is quite another.

This is where "the personal is the magical" comes in. Is your magical system an abstract Thing, etched in the sky? Or is it intended to work for actual human magical practitioners? Where groups are rejecting trans people or nonbinary people or queer people generally, they're fundamentally saying, "That's *just* personal."

When we ask queer people to behave "as if" they are not queer for the sake of a group's rules and customs, we're asking queer people to leave their identities outside. Like, it's okay to be queer—just keep it out of my ritual space.

The personal is the magical. And inclusivity matters. We can all—even queer people—do better.

Journal/Discussion Prompts

- Do you see your practice today as treating polarity "as it always was," as ignoring polarity, or something else?
- Has your view of polarity in p-word practice changed over time? Is it the same as what you first learned?

Chapter Five

How We Got Here, Part 1:
From Antiquity to the Renaissance

Before imposing a history lesson on an innocent reader, I think it's fair to ask why the history matters: What is there in the history of magical ideas that will help us today?

When I began researching polarity and its history, I wanted answers to some basic questions. First, what is polarity? As I asked this question, the second one became compelling: How did this "polarity" thing become the set of customs, traditions, and rules that the magical community has largely retained into the twenty-first century?

In Wicca, it is common for people to work in magical partnerships. Often those are mixed-gender partnerships, and in many covens such partnerships are *required*, and required to be mixed gender. Also, quite often, partners are not sexual couples, or don't have to be. To quote the Farrars: "It is…as completely removed from coitus, as ballroom dancing. Brother and sister, father and daughter, mother and son, can and do work this kind of magic together."[68]

---

68. Janet and Stewart Farrar, *Eight Sabbats for Witches*, 170.

So how did *that* happen? How did we get to the idea of asexual gender polarity partnerships? I had some ideas and started digging. Then I went further back. Then I had more questions.

In sum, my questions were:

- Where did the idea of polarity originate?
- Does polarity magic originate in or derive from sex magic or sexual ritual (especially the *hieros gamos*)?
- If so, when and how did the sex get removed?
- How did the idea of gender polarity get so incredibly abstract? How did we go from male and female to sun and moon?
- How did any or all of this turn into the modern concept of magical partnership?

In truth, I started merely with a bit of curiosity, but the more I explored, the more illuminating it was. What I discovered helped me understand the occult world in which I live and showed me a way forward. With a deeper understanding of polarity's underpinnings, section 2 of this book—which offers new ways of exploring polarities ritually and spiritually—became possible.

The Ancient World

The ancient philosophy of dualism is where we first see the concept of dividing reality into a male aspect and a female aspect.

The dualism of Plato (427–347 BCE) was concerned primarily with the split between body and soul. We can identify this split as "God" and "human," but "human" here is male. As described by Thomas Laqueur, the ancients understood humanity as fundamentally one gender.[69] Humans are perfect in the male form but imperfect in the female form. The phallus is perfection, while the womb is an inversion. Even biblically, we see the creation of humanity as the creation of man: Adam. Woman (Eve) is merely a companion (in one version anyway). The perception of one "true" gender

---

69. Laqueur, *Making Sex: Body and Gender from the Greeks to Freud.*

allows the high/low split to be assigned male/female easily. Male is that which is close to the divine, while female is that which is debased.

Plato identified matter as female and form as male. Form is the soul, the philosophical nature, the essence. Matter is the body, the container.[70] Aristotle (384–322 BCE), Plato's student, shifts the focus of dualism and gives us a lot of philosophical ideas about the essential nature of male and female. Aristotle understood the female as passive and material, and the male as active and moving. As Brandy Williams says:

> These precepts, that male and female are opposites, that the male is light and good, that the male provides the active form to female passive matter…were packaged by Aristotle and passed down the centuries to the theologians and academicians of later ages.[71]

Female, in Aristotle's worldview, is decidedly lesser; male gets intelligence, power, and the ability to act in the world. Later efforts to make these equal keep enough of the basic division so that patriarchy is never truly threatened. Woman's embodiment is seen as a source of power, but it is a motherly power, a passive power, and it cannot be activated in the world except by men.

We can understand these ancient philosophers as being concerned with the underpinnings of life. They wanted to know how life came into being and understand the nature of reality. What are things made of? What is their true nature? Dividing nature into these categories and classifications comes from the desire to understand.

From Aristotle, occultists inherit a great deal of classification. Greek philosophers were organizing and classifying things for hundreds of years before him, of course. Empedocles, Hippocrates, and Plato all contributed to the philosophy of the four elements of Air, Fire, Water, and Earth. Even today, we occultists busily correspond pretty much everything to the four elements. Aristotle also identified four *essences:* heat, cold, dryness, and

---

70. Ainsworth, "Form vs. Matter."

71. Williams, *The Woman Magician*, 74.

moistness. Fire is dry and hot, Water is wet and cold, Air is wet and hot, and Earth is dry and cold.[72] By identifying women as cold and men as hot, Aristotle tied all natural classifications to a gender dualism.

Hermeticism

The *Hermetica* were texts written around the third century CE by Hermes Trismegistus, a semi-mythological figure. It is from the portion known as the Emerald Tablet that we get the well-known occult philosophical principle "as above, so below" (or "that which is above is like to that which is below, and that which is below is like to that which is above"). Hermeticism, too, describes a duality between soul and matter, between heavenly truth and physical untruth.

The principles of Hermeticism influence almost every aspect of Western occultism, from alchemy to astrology, tarot to Theosophy, Rosicrucianism, Freemasonry, and ceremonial magic. Interestingly, we'll see that at least one bit of Hermetic philosophy, highly influential on understandings of polarity, actually originates in the twentieth century.[73]

The *Hermetica*'s dualism is that between God and humans, between the eternal divine and the ephemeral and material. The eternal is true, and the material is untrue. Thus, body, gender, and the like are fundamentally untrue. Hermetic researcher and mage Sam Block has this to say about gender and sexuality in Hermetics:

> There is nothing in the Hermetic texts…regarding much along the lines of sexuality…beyond a few high-level descriptions of biological reproduction in humans. It's important to remember that, in Hermeticism, there is no essential or divine notion of masculinity or femininity, and that the whole point of Hermetic doctrine is that you are not your body and the only thing that's of importance (from a Hermetic standpoint) is the soul, which is held to be androgyne/genderless, to say nothing of God likewise being androgyne/

---

72. Lipp, *The Way of Four,* 14.

73. Greer, "Source of *The Kybalion* in Anna Kingsford's Hermetic System."

queer. Hermeticism is quite amenable to being queered, if not already queer from the start depending on your interpretation of the texts.[74]

Alchemy

Alchemy comes to us shrouded in confusion. In part, this is entirely on purpose: alchemists wrote their lab notes in a kind of code, tangled in metaphor and pseudonyms. In part, confusion about alchemy might reflect a lack of scientific education; it all makes a lot more sense if you understand chemistry. In part, I think the mixture of science and spirituality is simply alien to us in our post-Enlightenment world.

But alchemy *is* understandable, and in many ways it is the key to unlocking the mysteries of polarity.

Alchemy is best understood as a magical process that reflects the Hermetic principle of "as above, so below." An alchemist worked in a laboratory to purify metals and other substances in order to achieve certain goals: most famously, the creation of the Philosopher's Stone, the magical substance that could bring immortality and healing. As alchemists worked on the microcosm—the metals and also their own souls—they understood themselves to be partaking in healing and perfecting the macrocosm—the world and all of creation. They were also bringing themselves closer to God by creating a more perfect, more Godlike version of nature.

Alchemy dates back to about 300 BCE, but the earliest known book on the subject arrived some six hundred years later: *Cheirokmeta* by Zosimos of Panopolis. At this time, around 300 CE, there was an incredible flowering of alchemy in the Egyptian city of Alexandria.

The alchemy of this period, and for many hundreds of years, followed the sulfur-mercury theory, which states that all metals are formed by a unique combination within the earth of sulfur and mercury. (Of course, here, "sulfur" and "mercury" are pseudonyms; creating gold is not nearly as easy as mixing sulfur and mercury, which actually creates cinnabar.)

---

74. Block, "Hermeticism FAQ: Part 1, Overview and History."

Sulfur is active and male; mercury is passive and female. We recognize this dualism from the Greeks, but alchemy's aims subvert the idea that duality is immutable. Rather than simply describing a duality, alchemy aims to transcend it by having the male and female interact. This is truly the first polarity magic.

In the lab, the alchemist separates a metal into its component parts by subjecting it to various treatments. It is burned, dissolved, and decayed. Its components are then separated and recombined in what is known as a "sacred marriage." (Other materials are introduced to force this process.) Next, through fermentation and distillation, the substance is again separated and purified. (Organic materials introduced in the "sacred marriage" are often the catalyst for fermentation, but sometimes chemical processes that work on metals are referred to as fermentation by the alchemist.) The final recombination is the end result of alchemy. It is also the union of opposites—the *coniunctio oppositorum*—that transcends polarity. (The entire process is known as the Great Work—*magnum opus*.)

Gendered language permeates alchemy, always with the intention of separating the poles in order to bring them together and create oneness. The combination of sulfur and mercury in a sacred marriage creates a hermaphrodite.[75] The famed alchemist Miriam (or Maria) the Jewess said, "Join the male and the female, and you will find what is sought."[76] Alchemical art shows mercury and sulfur, female and male, as two figures in bed together, finally becoming a two-headed, two-sexed being, the *rebis* (divine hermaphrodite), the end result of the alchemical process.

In alchemy, though, the gender of the components is always metaphorical and never embodied. The closest alchemy gets to sex magic is in its rather explicit illustrations. The gendered body of the alchemist is never a factor in the work; male and female alchemists do exactly the same thing in the lab.

---

75. *Hermaphrodite* is considered an offensive term and should not be used to describe an intersex human being. However, it is also the historically accurate term for alchemical processes and will be used in that context.

76. Patai, *The Jewish Alchemists*, 66.

A third, mediating force was added to sulfur and mercury by the renowned alchemist Paracelsus, whose *Opus Paramirum* was published in 1530. In it, Paracelsus defines the "three primes" (*tria prima*) of sulfur, mercury, and salt. (Today, some students of alchemy work with the three primes, while others adhere to the original sulfur-mercury theory.)

The addition of salt doesn't mean that Paracelsus's alchemy was not based on polarity. Rather, salt is a "third" in the sense described in chapter 2. It mediates between the poles and unites them. Male soul/sulfur and female spirit/mercury are grounded in the body that is salt.

Inner work was always a part of alchemy. The condition of the alchemist's spirit was considered a key factor in the Great Work. The belief was that an alchemist seeking to become closer to God could create gold in the laboratory, but an alchemist seeking gold out of greed could not. Separating science from spirit was a product of the Age of Reason centuries later, so prayer and meditation were as much a part of an alchemist's scientific work as retorts and alembics.

By the nineteenth century, the whole thing seemed a little wacky, and very *un*reasonable in the Age of Reason. For those studying magic, though, alchemy was there in the underpinnings. It was part of Cornelius Agrippa's *Three Books of Occult Philosophy* for one, and in the *Hermetica*, Hermes Trismegistus called alchemy one of the "three parts of wisdom" (the other two being astrology and magic). These were and are core magical texts. So what's an occultist to do?

At this point, psychological and spiritual alchemy step in.

Here, the idea is that the inner work is the *entire* work of alchemy; the lab is the self and the transmutation into gold is the elevation of the soul. In 1850, the esotericist Mary Anne Atwood published *A Suggestive Inquiry into the Hermetic Mystery*, which is the beginning of the idea that alchemy is a purely spiritual exercise. Nearly a hundred years later, Carl Jung published *Psychology and Alchemy*, nudging the subject from the purely spiritual into the psychological.

By the way, Jung seemed to believe that the records of alchemical experimentation were essentially hallucinations:

While working on his chemical experiments the operator had certain psychic experiences which appeared to him as the particular behaviour of the chemical process. Since it was a question of projection, he was naturally unconscious of the fact that the experience had nothing to do with matter itself (that is, with matter as we know it today). He experienced his projection as a property of matter; but what he was in reality experiencing was his own unconscious.[77]

"Appeared to him" sounds pretty dismissive to me, as if Jung is saying that the alchemist merely imagined the physical outcomes of alchemy. That's pretty much the way magic is treated by "reasonable" people in a nutshell.

The Queerness of Alchemy

One of alchemy's most important founders is a woman. Miriam the Jewess invented laboratory equipment still in use today. By the Middle Ages, misogyny kept women out of the lab, but that was the cultural misogyny of the time, not something built into alchemy. We can look at the gender polarity of alchemy—metaphorical, not misogynist, not reliant on a physical definition of gender or sex—to see what it has to teach us. As we apply alchemy to the mind and spirit, as had begun during the occult revival of the nineteenth century, this is even more significant.

In an earlier work, I wrote:

At its heart, alchemy takes something (the world, the self, a metal, or plant) apart and puts it back together in a holier and more perfect form. Through a series of stages, that something is destroyed, separated into its component parts, each of which is perfected, and then reintegrated. The parts are elements or polarities (at least metaphorically gendered), but through the alchemical process, separation is shown to be an illusion: Genders are really the divine hermaphrodite, the snake swallows its own tail, and transcendence is achieved.[78]

77. Jung, *Psychology and Alchemy*, para. 46.

78. Lipp, *The Beginner's Guide to the Occult*, 94.

The *magnum opus* of spiritual alchemy goes something like this: We face some kind of crisis, something that can either destroy us or force us to change. This "dissolution" gives us the opportunity to take ourselves apart, to look at each piece of ourselves. In alchemy, gender is inherently a part of this. Looking at everything within me, including my maleness and my femaleness, I can determine which parts are dross and can be discarded, leaving a purer form of me. The next step is "coagulation," putting it all back together. My purified, examined, and accepted self is reborn. This process is called *solve et coagula*, dissolve and coagulate.

To me, *solve et coagula* is genuinely one of the queerest processes in all of magic. The description sounds like coming out, and it sounds like gender transition. Certainly I have trans friends and relatives in the magical community who understand their own transition as *solve et coagula*. I cannot help but think that the great occult author, comic book writer, and trans woman Rachel Pollack had something like this in mind when she named the first trans character in comic books *Coagula*.[79]

Taking apart my inner gender(s), burning away the parts that don't fit, and bringing it all back together newly as a divinely intersex being is a radical way of understanding polarity, and yet that radical perception has been available since the year 300 CE.

Allow me to digress for a personal anecdote. I have had this project—a book on polarity—in the back of my mind for several years, but I could never really get my arms around it. Then, while writing *The Beginner's Guide to the Occult*, I needed to study alchemy. There's one kind of study where you read a book or two. I'd done that in the past. There's a whole 'nother kind where you have to write about it. When I finally felt I understood alchemy, all of a sudden the polarity book (this book) just *popped*. I suddenly knew that I could write about this subject, because the queer, transformational, subversive nature of polarity was there in antiquity, just waiting to be explored.

---

79. Pollack tells me she's not sure how much this was a conscious idea at the time, but since the connection between this concept in alchemy and transition is "perfect," she's happy to be credited. Coagula first appeared in *Doom Patrol* #70 in 1993.

Alchemy is one of the primary magical disciplines underlying Western occultism today. Rarely practiced, it is still deeply influential, and its impact on our study of polarity is obvious. Separating the poles in order to bring them together to achieve a magical or spiritual goal is *exactly* our definition of polarity from chapter 1. The polarity of alchemy is rarely understood as radical and queer, but that understanding is readily available from studying even the oldest materials. As we move forward in our examination of the history of polarity in magic, this radicalism and queerness should be kept in mind—particularly as other cultural forces move to crush it.

Kabbalah

The hard part of discussing Kabbalah is that it can be really off-putting to readers less familiar with the Tree of Life. It can seem like a string of unfamiliar foreign words and phrases: Malkuth, sephirot, Shekhinah, blah blah blah. It's easy for your eyes to glaze over.

But a huge part of how we understand polarity today comes directly from Kabbalah, or passes through Kabbalah on its way to us. The Tree of Life is a structured set of polarities flowing through all of creation, with a great deal of mysticism, symbolism, correspondences, and power attached. While these correspondences are gendered, they also transcend gender. If we could unhook the cultural baggage from ideas like "force and form" or "compassion and strength," we'd find knowledge and magic in them that are genuinely transformative. *Can* we unhook them? I think so, but it remains an open question. First, though, we have to dive into the facts a bit, unfamiliar foreign words and all.

Which Kabbalah?

When we talk about Kabbalah, we need to specify which Kabbalah we mean. The *Sefir Yetzirah* dates from maybe 200 BCE (or maybe some other period—it's unclear) and is the oldest Kabbalistic text. We're boldly skipping right past it to the *Zohar*, written in the latter half of the thirteenth century.[80]

---

80. Moses de Leon claimed he "found" the manuscript and that it was written in the first century CE by Simeon ben Yohai. Some Jewish sources accept this claim, or accept that a central core of the *Zohar* may be that old and de Leon added to it. But I just can't with miraculously discovered documents. I just can't.

Why skip ahead? In part, because the *Sefir Yetzirah* doesn't deal with polarity in the way that the *Zohar* does, and it is gendered differently. The *Sefir Yetzirah* is more feminine and is based more in threes: not just a polarity plus a third, as we've discussed and as we'll see in the *Zohar*, but triplicities as themselves. There are plenty of polarities and dualities in the *Sefir Yetzirah*, but the theme of three is more prevalent. Further, the sephirot of the *Sefir Yetzirah* don't have an obvious correspondence to those in the *Zohar*'s more well-known Tree of Life; different Jewish scholars assign the correspondence from *Sefir Yetzirah* to *Zohar* differently, and at least some think they're not even the same mystical system (thus explaining the lack of a readily apparent one-to-one correspondence).[81] Meanwhile, the *Zohar* is the source of the Tree of Life glyph commonly used in modern occultism, so it is influential in the occultism we know today, and it is encoded as polarity from head to toe (or from Crown to Kingdom). While the Tree of Life is a part of both Jewish mysticism and secular occultism, the *Sefir Yetzirah* is confined largely to Judaism, and thus is less meaningful to our work here.

Kabbalistic Influence and Influences on Kabbalah

Although we can think of medieval Jewish communities as segregated and isolated—they are, after all, where the word *ghetto* comes from—the Jewish sages of that era were sophisticated students of mysticism and philosophy. They studied alchemy, Hermetics, and Gnosticism. The influence of earlier philosophies permeates Kabbalah—in fact, astrology is built into the *Sefir Yetzirah*. That's important for us as we trace these ideas from antiquity to the present day. Kabbalah doesn't represent a separate component so much as a next significant step.

Historically, the Kabbalah is crucial; it's as fundamental to modern magical thinking as alchemy, even when (as in the case of alchemy) practitioners have *no idea* they're being influenced by its hidden presence. From the *Zohar* in the thirteenth century, the Kabbalah was picked up by Christians and

---

81. Hammer, *Return to the Place: The Magic, Meditation, and Mystery of Sefer Yetzirah.*

Hermeticists, often with anti-Semitic intention ("let's get this beautiful mysticism away from the unworthy Jews who created it," basically). By the fifteenth century, Kabbalah was incorporated into Agrippa's *Three Books of Occult Philosophy*, which remains influential even today. From Agrippa, it worked its way to the Golden Dawn and then…well, we'll get to that.

Sexuality, Polarity, and Kabbalah

One historical question we started with was how did polarity get so abstract, and that led us to alchemy. Another is how sex, and sexual ritual, is connected to that abstract polarity, and that's where Kabbalah comes in.

As mentioned, alchemy is gendered and polar but not sexual or embodied. When we turn our attention to Kabbalah though, the sex definitely gets sexier.

This isn't necessarily visible at first glance, but as mentioned in chapter 3, sexual union of God and his bride, his Shekhinah, as a mystical goal of Kabbalah is ever-present. While the sexuality of God is metaphorical, with union meant to be understood as a healing of nature and the world so that it can be in its ideal and holy state, we've seen that it nevertheless translates into the sexual union of a human couple.

The medieval Kabbalistic sages were part of a deeply patriarchal culture whose studies excluded women. Women were not privy to the knowledge that marital sex was part of *tikkun olam*—healing the world. But it was (and is).

So it's the thirteenth century and women are forbidden from entering alchemical labs not because of alchemy but because the culture is sexist. (It still is today, but we're allowed in labs now.) The study of Kabbalah is 100 percent the business of men; women make babies and men study. Again, this has nothing to do with Kabbalah itself and everything to do with the culture that surrounds it.

We can wonder if the lusty imagery of the Kabbalah was another motivation for male mystics to keep women away from the Kabbalah—maybe the great sages didn't want women reading their porn. Judaism, then and now, places value on marital pleasure and on women's pleasure; sex is a sacred duty, and a husband's job is to please his wife. As we saw in chapter 3, this sacred duty is also a manifestation of polarity magic, but this information was kept from women for centuries.[82]

Gender Polarity Symbolism in the Kabbalah

When we look at the Tree of Life, we see a series of pairs with a connected third. Each pair is a polarity, and each third is the meeting of that polarity to create a synthesis that represents a perfect joining of the pair. It gets more complex, as we'll see.

The gender correspondences on the Tree of Life are also complex. Today, many Kabbalists will tell you that the female sephirot are Binah and Malkut, and the rest are male. This despite the fact that the word *sephirah* itself is feminine, as are several of the names of individual sephirot. Chokmah (Wisdom), for example, is called the Supernal Father, but the word is feminine, and Philo of Alexandria, at the turn of the last millennium, documented that God is the husband of Wisdom.[83] Gevurah, too, is a feminine word, as is Yesod.

In the Kabbalah, creation flows from the infinite to the specific. The sephirot are known as "emanations"; they are emanating from God in an interactive flow that eventually yields creation as we know it. This flow is one of polarities interacting and then resolving, bit by bit, until they finally resolve as manifested reality.

Each specific moment is intensely itself and cannot create without interacting with its counterpart. Chokmah is *force*, the driving forward of creative energy. But Chokmah by itself is indiscriminate and without shape. Chokmah requires the next sephirah, Binah (Understanding). Binah, the Supernal Mother, is *form*, giving shape to Chokmah's force. Together, they create the invisible sephirah, Da'at (Knowledge), and their united force and form permeate the Tree until we reach Malkut.

Here is the gender polarity of the Kabbalah in a nutshell. The creative spark emanates from Keter, the Crown, pure potentiality. From here, each pair is unbalanced without the other, and each pair creates a perfect unity.

---

82. In some Chasidic and ultra-Orthodox Jewish communities, this information is still kept from women.

83. Patai, *The Hebrew Goddess*, 98.

We can see this in the illustration of the Tree of Life, which is three triangles with Malkut (the Kingdom of manifestation) standing beneath. Each triangle is a pair and its synthesis: Chokmah and Binah synthesized in Da'at and synthesized by Keter;[84] Chesed and Gevurah synthesized in Tiferet; Netzach and Hod synthesized in Yesod; and all of them feeding into Malkut.

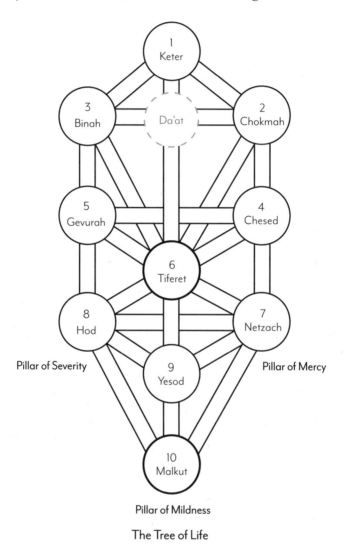

The Tree of Life

---

84. The Supernal Triangle of the Tree of Life is Keter, Binah, and Chokmah, but at the top of the Tree, there's a second triangle formed with Da'at.

In each case, the gender politics are odious. The male provides kindness, energy, and compassion, while the female provides darkness, stasis, and severity.

The Kabbalah gives us a lot to work with. There are these three polarities and their synthesis, and reams and reams and reams of brilliant magical, philosophical, and mystical writing about them. The Kabbalah provides a library's worth of meditations and explorations.

But there's that odious gender politics. Or is there?

The vertical running down the left side of the Tree is called the Pillar of Severity; it is headed by Binah and is considered female. The right side is the Pillar of Mercy, headed by Chokmah and considered male. In the center are the synthesizing, mediating, and elevating sephirot: the Pillar of Mildness. The center pillar is the location of those sephirot that function as a meeting place between their "parent" sephirot. The Pillar of Mildness is not gendered, and its meeting of polarities is a powerful place for nonbinary occultists to explore.

As we discussed in chapter 3 though, Tiferet is male, while Malkut is female, and they are meant to be sexually united. Jewish ritual and prayer send sacred energy toward this spiritual-sexual union. Yet Tiferet and Malkut are both on the Pillar of Mildness, so while they are gendered, they are at the same time not gendered, or perhaps are intersex, like the *rebis* of alchemy. (I should note that many early Kabbalists were alchemists, and at least one Kabbalistic text, the *Esh M'tzaref*, sought to combine the two, corresponding the sephirot to metals, with Malkut being the Philosopher's Stone.[85])

So the sacred marriage of Tiferet and Malkut is both heteronormative and completely gender-bending. They are male (Tiferet) and female (Malkut), but neither male nor female (because they're on the nongendered pillar), or both male and female (because both the preceding are true). Tiferet is male but is also the "third" created by Chesed and Gevurah. Malkut is female but is also the manifestation of *all* the polar energies of the Tree.

---

85. Sledge, "Kabbalah + Alchemy + Magic – The Refiner's Fire – שׁ מצרף – Transmutation & Jewish Mystical Theurgy."

Netzach and Hod manifest Yesod, and Yesod's energy flows into Malkut, into created reality. Yesod, the meeting place between Tiferet and Malkut, is also a "third" and not gendered, or is intersex.

As noted in chapter 3, the sacred marriage is sometimes described as between Yesod and Malkut. *Yesod* is a female noun in Hebrew and corresponds to a feminine Moon in Hermetic Kabbalah, but it's also a euphemism for *penis* in songs and poems about the sacred marriage:

> Right and left, and the bride in between
> Comes forth in her jewels and sumptuous raiments.
> Her husband embraces her, and with her Yesod,
> Which gives her pleasure, he presses her mightily.[86]

(Excuse me, I'm a little faint.)

So Yesod is either the meeting place of the Bride and King, or it is the King himself, and/or it is the penis, and it is also a feminine word, and also a planet with feminine correspondence.

I want to back away from all these specifics (which have certainly put some readers to sleep) to say this: *the core act of polarity sex magic in the Kabbalah is genderqueer.*

Journal/Discussion Prompts

- How do you think occult history has influenced your practice? Do you see in it traces of alchemy? Of Kabbalah?

---

86. Patai, *The Hebrew Goddess*, 272–73. Patai explains that the man's penis is "hers" because it reunites God with his bride. Not being an expert on Hebrew poetry, I can only imagine other readings are possible.

Chapter Six

How We Got Here, Part 2: From the Western Magical Tradition to Today

The Western magical tradition inherited the entire magical and philosophical history of the West to that point. Hermetics, alchemy, and the magic of the Greeks, Hebrews, and Egyptians all spilled into the cauldron of the grimoire tradition and other forms of medieval and Renaissance magic in the West, creating a magical stew that emerged during the occult revival of the nineteenth century.

The grimoire tradition began around the twelfth century. Following Agrippa's *Three Books of Occult Philosophy*, magic became markedly more Hermetic and more Kabbalistic. This means that magical symbols, tools, and ceremonies all acquired correspondences that were polar, and often gendered.

Three Books of Occult Philosophy spearheaded, and exemplifies, the amalgamation of the magical and philosophical streams that became the Western magic we have today. Francis Barrett's *The Magus*, published in 1801, lifted much of *Three Books of Occult Philosophy* wholesale. It became hugely influential during the occult revival and was considered foundational for the Golden Dawn. Quoting Brandy Williams:

Our magic directly descends from Hellenistic magic. Rituals pre-
served in the Greek Magical Papyri can be performed by the educated
magician today. These magical texts blended Egyptian and Greek
magic with bits of surviving Babylonian lore and early alchemy, and
Gnostic insights combined with neo-Platonic philosophy and Helle-
nized Judaism.[87]

The magic of the West, then, inherited ideas of dualism from Plato,
Aristotle, Neoplatonism, and so on. It picked up abstractions about gender from alchemy, as well as ideas about separating and merging gendered
abstractions: polarity. In Kabbalah, we find an expression of polarity that
almost excludes all other forces. The universe itself depends on the polar
flow of energies. Author David Ariel describes this dependence: "Alone,
the polarities…remain ineffectual. A universe of extremes cannot endure.
All opposites need to be moderated by another element in order to be
brought into a state of harmony and balance."[88]

The occult revival was the fertile soil in which this mixture was planted.
I think one of the meaningful things about this revival, which is rarely discussed, is that it occurred during the Victorian era. If I say "Victorian era"
conversationally, you probably know I'm talking about sexually repressed
and rigid mores and, in fact, the origin of many specific sexual taboos
(unless you think I'm talking about ornate and overcrowded home decor, I
guess). Yet I rarely see occultists question how the Victorian milieu might
have impacted occultism.

From the Enlightenment onward, we can expect the model of two
genders that we know today to be the assumption, even though the one-
gender model discussed previously, still influences thinking about what is
male and what is female. With a two-gender model comes the idea that the
sexes are separate but equal. Polarity depends on both in balance, and can
be seen as empowering of women. It's certainly empowering by compari-
son, but the division leaves women on the passive pole, waiting around for
male activation.

---

87. Williams, *The Woman Magician*, 47.

88. Ariel, *The Mystic Quest*, 80.

As with the sexism of medieval Kabbalism, we have to understand the occult revival as part of its surrounding culture. Occultists then and now like to see themselves as outsiders and not influenced by conventional society, but that's simply not true. Nineteenth- and early-twentieth-century occultists assumed homophobia was inherent in polarity magic, but surely ancient Greek magicians did not! Neopagans of the 1970s were likely to think that sexual freedom was built into occult philosophy, but by the 1990s that attitude was far less prevalent. It's much easier to understand this "change" in Pagan morality if you see it as merely a reflection of what was going on everywhere in the culture in which those Pagans lived.

Often we see "new" sexual or gender freedoms as not really that free in retrospect. I'm often reminded of the Harvey Girls.[89] Today, we might look at young women living strictly controlled lives in dormitories for low wages as patriarchal control of women—and we'd be right. But in the 1880s, working for the Harvey restaurants allowed young women a freedom to leave home and strike out on their own. It was an independent option that wasn't marriage or sex work and allowed single women to travel unchaperoned to new places while still being seen as "decent."

The Hermetic Order of the Golden Dawn

European occultism prior to the Enlightenment usually excluded women. Magical lodges were generally all male. During the occult revival, women began to emerge as powerful forces. The founding of the Isis-Urania Temple of the Golden Dawn in 1888 was a breakthrough in occultism generally and for the inclusion of women in particular. At one point, a woman—Florence Farr—took over leadership of the Golden Dawn in England when Moina and S. L. MacGregor Mathers moved to Paris. Naturally, women's leadership was resisted: "one lodge was specifically formed so that the men in it would not be obliged to report to a woman."[90]

We can see that women were integrated into the Golden Dawn in ways that were not gender-specific: as writers, leaders, and so on. But roles were

---

89. Knece, "Who Were the Harvey Girls?"

90. Williams, *The Woman Magician*, 61, quoting Alex Owen, *The Place of Enchantment: British Occultism and the Culture of the Modern*.

also created that were specifically for women. In ritual, women played the role of goddesses and priestesses, while men performed the role of gods and priests, and polarity magic was part of the higher "orders" (levels of initiation). The third order (essentially the highest level) of the Golden Dawn taught "alchemy and spiritual sexuality."[91]

Women were prominent as creative forces, leaders, financiers, and inspiration, yet like the Harvey Girls, they were hemmed in by the restrictions of their culture.[92] The magical polarity, the veneration of goddesses as well as gods, and the sexual attitudes were all tinged by Victorian attitudes.

This matters to us because the extraordinary magic and ritual of the Golden Dawn and its many offshoots uses a gender-essentialist, patriarchal, and usually homophobic polarity paradigm. Yet, as we've seen, there's a historically queer underpinning to polarity. When we understand that it's the culture and not the magic itself that restricts our understanding of polarity, we're freed of the belief that polarity is inherently, well, Victorian.

One of the odd ways in which the Victorian attitude manifested was as an obsession with purity and celibacy. While it is normal for some people to choose celibate relationships, it seems hard to believe that so many prominent members of one magical order should just happen to make that choice. Moina and MacGregor Mathers's marriage was celibate, for example, and Maud Gonne's relationship with William Butler Yeats was plagued by a need for "purity" conflicting with sexual desire. Aleister Crowley's work with sex magic was one of the reasons he was disdained by, and eventually split with, the Golden Dawn. The historical record shows an organization using gender polarity with an erotic undercurrent, teaching sexual mysteries at the highest degrees but also suppressing any actual sex. It's no wonder tensions ran high!

The gender polarity of the Golden Dawn became a blueprint for the place of women and what was defined as women's energy in Western magical traditions generally. The Golden Dawn ends up with its fingerprints all over just about every magical group that followed. Groups that

91. Denisoff, "The Hermetic Order of the Golden Dawn, 1888–1901."
92. See Greer, *Women of the Golden Dawn.*

came out of the Golden Dawn include (but are not limited to) the A∴A∴, Thelemic orders (such as the O.T.O. from the time of Aleister Crowley's leadership), the Society of the Inner Light (see below), the Fellowship of the Rosy Cross, and the Builders of the Adytum (BOTA). Each of these, in turn, has had offshoots or students who went on to form other magical groups. So the Golden Dawn influence, even when faint, spread throughout Western magic, and its ideas on gender and polarity were part of that.

The Kybalion

I use the word *influential* a lot. In my forty-some years in the occult community, I've found that there are many ideas and practices that seem ubiquitous but are often unsourced. They just "are." Yet many times it turns out such ideas come from *one* book, *one* teacher, *one* source, *one* person's good idea. While this good idea becomes widespread, its origins often seem to disappear. Thus, there are certain books and documents that few occultists have read, yet their influence is massive; their fingerprints are everywhere. *The Kybalion* is one such hand—fingerprints everywhere, original source forgotten.

Published in 1908 anonymously by "Three Initiates," the book asserts that it is an explanation and expansion on an ancient text by Hermes Trismegistus known as *The Kybalion*. (No such ancient text exists.) Its ubiquity is such that it can actually be hard to locate real, original Hermetics in twentieth- and twenty-first-century occult texts, as so many are actually the falsified texts from this work. It's important to emphasize that, despite its claims, *The Kybalion* has virtually nothing to do with ancient Hermetics, the *Hermetica*, or Hermes Trismegistus.

The Kybalion outlines the "Seven Hermetic Principles," claiming that the entire Hermetic philosophy is based on them. They are:

1. The Principle of Mentalism
2. The Principle of Correspondence
3. The Principle of Vibration
4. The Principle of Polarity
5. The Principle of Rhythm

6. The Principle of Cause and Effect

7. The Principle of Gender

These principles are important to our study for a couple of reasons. The first is because they define gender and polarity principles. Surprisingly to me when I first read them, they're separate principles, which we'll explore shortly.

The second reason is because these principles seemed to permeate Western occultism during the crucial period of the late nineteenth and early twentieth centuries. For example, *The Secret Doctrine of the Rosicrucians* lists the "Seven Cosmic Principles" as:

I. The Principle of Correspondence

II. The Principle of Law and Order

III. The Principle of Vibration

IV. The Principle of Rhythm

V. The Principle of Cycles

VI. The Principle of Polarity

VII. The Principle of Sex

The order of the Seven Cosmic Principles is different from that of the Seven Hermetic Principles, they're "cosmic" instead of "Hermetic," and it's "sex" instead of "gender," but we can understand these two sets of principles, in context, as pretty much the same.[93] Not surprisingly, the anonymous authors of both works are widely said to be the same man: William Walker Atkinson, a New Thought teacher and writer.[94]

Dion Fortune's first teacher, Theodore Moriarty, included Seven Cosmic Principles identical to those above in *The Mystery of Man*, published around 1924. This book is considered to be a huge influence on Fortune's own *The Cosmic Doctrine* (1949).

---

93. Although we often distinguish between sex and gender today, we can be confident that the intention in 1908 was to treat them as equivalent.

94. Chapel, "The Kybalion's New Clothes."

The Principle of Polarity

The supposed "original" *Kybalion* text goes like this:

> Everything is Dual; everything has poles; everything has its pair of
> opposites; like and unlike are the same; opposites are identical in
> nature, but different in degree; extremes meet; all truths are but
> half-truths; all paradoxes may be reconciled.[95]

The text goes on to discuss the idea that opposites are actually the
same, using examples such as temperature. Heat and cold are opposites,
but there isn't an absolute point where something is cold or hot; it's per-
ceptual and relative—both are merely measurements of the same thing.
Other pairs used as illustrations of this principle are large and small, light
and darkness, and high and low. Positive and negative are included as well.

It's helpful to note that the text doesn't say everything *is a pole,* just that
everything is *polar.* It's not that you or I are a specific pole with an opposite,
but rather that we're on a scale that has opposite poles. That is, if the two
ends of a pole are black and white, there's no assumption that everything is
either black or white; every possible shade of gray exists on the spectrum
between those poles. Implicitly, we're all on many such scales, perhaps an
infinite number.

The ideas of magic found in this text include that anything can be
changed by changing its polarity, but things can't switch classification, so
that magic can change heat to cold but not heat to darkness.

The Principle of Gender

Here, the supposed "original" *Kybalion* text says:

> Gender is in everything; everything has its Masculine and Feminine
> Principles; Gender manifests on all planes.[96]

The exposition goes on to say:

---

95. Three Initiates, *The Kybalion*, 1912, Chapter 2.
96. Three Initiates, *The Kybalion*, 1912, Chapter 2.

The Principle of Gender works ever in the direction of generation, regeneration, and creation. Everything, and every person, contains the two Elements or Principles, or this great Principle, within it, him or her. Every Male thing has the Female Element also; every Female contains also the Male Principle.[97]

The Kybalion is definitely opposed to equating this "lofty" principle with sex or lust or anything smutty. Heavens, no! It goes on to describe "the latest" science about electricity, corresponding the negative to the female and the positive to the male, correcting the reader's misconceptions about negative (turns out that it's really active and good), and expressing confidence that science will continue to align with Hermetics. Although *The Kybalion* states that God is beyond gender, it allows that you can consider God the Father and male, while Nature is the Mother and female.

The text itself doesn't make a one-to-one connection between the Principle of Gender and the Principle of Polarity. In fact, they seem to contradict each other. The Principle of Polarity here says that things that are opposite are fundamentally the same, and there are many, maybe infinite, gradients between them. Contrarily, the text treats masculine and feminine as fixed. There's definitely no acknowledgment of gender fluidity or of states that aren't fully one gender or the other.

In moving forward toward the future, *The Kybalion's* Principle of Polarity can be a useful touchpoint, but its Principle of Gender is locked into an outmoded essentialism. Usefully, *The Kybalion* separates gender and polarity for us, so that as we explore polarity, we don't ever have to think of it as inherently gendered.

Aleister Crowley and Dion Fortune

In the post-Victorian magical world, Dion Fortune and Aleister Crowley constitute two sides of the same coin. Both were from the same magical milieu and both were prolific writers and teachers as well as talented magicians, formed organizations that are alive today, and had seemingly oppo-

---

97. Three Initiates, *The Kybalion*, 1912, Chapter 2.

site ideas. It's easy to understand these two as the greatest occultists of their era. Both heavily emphasized sex magic, although Fortune spoke of purity and Crowley was well known as a libertine.

Both Crowley and Fortune were products of the Golden Dawn. Crowley was an initiate of S. L. MacGregor Mathers, while Fortune was a member of Alpha et Omega, one of the earliest Golden Dawn offshoots, and worked closely with Moina Mathers. Both worked deeply with Kabbalah and with ideas about polarity, gender, and sex. There is no Western magical organization or philosophy extant today that doesn't carry at least a trace of influence from one or both of these giants.

Thelema and Aleister Crowley

Aleister Crowley was one of the great religious adepts as well as a controversial figure in many ways, not least because of his bisexuality and use of drugs and sex in magic. His magical background included Freemasonry, initiation into the Adeptus Minor grade of the Golden Dawn, the practice of Enochian magic and Goetia, as well as studying Hindu and Islamic mysticism and Egyptian magic.

In 1904, while Crowley was on his honeymoon in Cairo, Egypt, his bride, Rose Kelly, entered a trance wherein she was contacted by a being called Aiwass, a messenger of the god Horus. For three days, Aiwass, through Kelly, dictated *The Book of the Law,* with Crowley as the scribe. Brandy Williams sees the influence of this on Crowley's magical work for the rest of his life, as well as on *The Book of the Law:*

> *The Book of the Law* among other things spoke to Crowley as the priest and scribe, and also referred to a female counterpart to the priest, the Scarlet Woman. Throughout his life Crowley sought a physical Scarlet Woman to partner with him in his magical explorations.[98]

The new Pagan religion that grew out of *The Book of the Law* was Thelema. In 1910 Crowley joined, and quickly took over, the O.T.O. (Ordo

---

98. Williams, *The Woman Magician*, 51.

Templi Orientis), making Thelema its basis.[99] He wrote the Gnostic Mass in 1913, and this became the core ritual of Thelema, although, according to O.T.O. expert and Crowley biographer Richard Kaczynski, "there's no evidence that Crowley himself ever celebrated the Mass in its entirety."[100]

The role of Priestess and Priest in the Gnostic Mass is overflowing with sexual symbolism. According to Lon Milo DuQuette:

> The two main officers responsible for consecrating the Host and Wine of the Eucharist portray and embody the Goddess Nuit (the Egyptian Goddess of the infinite night sky), and Hadit (the winged-God of the infinite Center of Nuit). This is the polarity designation for this particular operation.
>
> The Goddess and the God 'marry' and the annihilatory *ecstasy* of their discharge climax *consecrates* the Host and Wine and transforms them into the *Child* of their union.[101]

The Gnostic Mass has five officers: Priest, Priestess, Deacon, and two Children. The Priest and Priestess were and are male and female roles. From the beginning, these roles were assumed to be based on "biological sex," and naturally no one performing the Mass in the 1930s, '40s, or '50s was thinking about trans or nonbinary identity. As DuQuette puts it:

> The officer designated in the ritual as *Priestess* assumes the role of the Goddess *Nuit*, and the officer designated in the ritual as Priest assumes the role of the God Hadit. While the personal gender or gender identification of the individuals may vary, the *roles* of the two deities they magically embody should remain unambiguously consistent with those of a potential mother and father.[102]

---

99. Lipp, *The Beginner's Guide to the Occult*, 128.

100. Richard Kaczynski, personal correspondence, October 14, 2021.

101. Lon Milo DuQuette, personal correspondence, October 6, 2021. DuQuette is a noted expert on the O.T.O. and Crowley, and as of this writing, he is the O.T.O.'s United States Deputy Grand Master.

102. Lon Milo DuQuette, personal correspondence, October 6, 2021.

There is neither polarity nor gender assigned to the other three roles. Early performances of the Mass included both men and women in the Deacon role, according to Richard Kaczynski.[103] Kaczynski adds, while being respectful of his oath of secrecy as an O.T.O. initiate, that there are "some gendered or gender-polar aspects in some other O.T.O. rituals."

Dion Fortune

It's hard to underestimate the level to which Fortune's work has touched the occult. Her direct influence is present, of course, in the occult organization she founded, the Society of the Inner Light, and its offshoot, the Avalon Group, founded by Gareth Knight. Broadly, her ideas are found throughout the Western Mystery Traditions, are all over Wicca, and show up in a variety of other occult spaces. As with *The Kybalion*, you need never have heard of Dion Fortune or read her works to be working a system shaped by her in some way, and this is especially true of ideas about polarity, gender, and magical partnership.

As far as I have been able to determine, it's Fortune who first published the idea that a magical group should have a balance of the sexes, and that a magical partnership between people of different sexes was necessary for certain work and that it need not be a physical relationship:

> The greatest importance is attached to the cooperation of male and female forces in any work involving practical occultism. In certain orders it is the custom to keep the lodge-membership evenly balanced between the sexes…
>
> …The male vehicle is positive and the female negative, and therefore the practical occultist finds that for certain types of work it is necessary to function in partnership or polarity, for only thus can a circuit be set up and a flow of cosmic force be induced.[104]

Fortune was a Theosophist, a member of Alpha et Omega, and eventually the founder of the Fraternity of the Inner Light (which became the

---

103. Richard Kaczynski, personal correspondence, October 14, 2021.

104. Fortune, *The Esoteric Philosophy of Love and Marriage*, 73.

Society of the Inner Light after her death). She was definitely influenced by *The Kybalion*, as described above.

The Esoteric Philosophy of Love and Marriage is one of Fortune's earliest works and is little known today,[105] yet this book contains the seeds of a lot of our understanding of occult polarity. In her allusion to "certain lodges," we can guess that she didn't invent these ideas,[106] yet only Fortune can be fairly credited with their dissemination.

The Esoteric Philosophy of Love and Marriage lays out an understanding of gender polarity that assumes polarity energy exists merely by two gendered people being present. It acknowledges that all humans are both male and female, but it strongly asserts that one's biological sex is a function of one's higher purpose; you *must* enact the "negative" female pole if you are female because that is why you were incarnated in a female body. Over and over, the book emphasizes the power of polarity work and its essentially non-erotic nature. It is also extravagantly homophobic, calling same-sex love "evil" and yet acknowledging that it is magically quite powerful. The idea is that, since a gay couple can call forth nonpolar energy, that energy is never grounded and so is available for magic. The funny part is that in seeking to explain why it's evil, she resorts to saying that it's basically pretty great except that, well, it's evil. Perfect circular logic.

These ideas, published in 1924, remain visible in Fortune's later works, including *The Mystical Qabalah*, a highly regarded and widely read book.

Wicca

Without attempting to squeeze too much history into too small a space, we can understand that the religion of Wicca as we know it today comes to us largely through Gerald Gardner. Gardner was initiated into the New Forest coven; adapted, added to, or wholly rewrote their rituals; sought

---

105. Dion Fortune is most famous for *The Mystical Qabalah*—her masterpiece—and for the novels *The Sea Priestess* and *Moon Magic*.

106. Fortune claimed that Moina Mathers kicked her out of Alpha et Omega for publishing secrets in this book, the implication being that she published sex magic secrets. Fortune contended, though, that she hadn't achieved the degree at which such secrets were revealed, and she attained the knowledge elsewhere. Magical orders and infighting!

publicity for the "witch-cult" (often to the chagrin of his fellow witches); and was first among those who helped create the movement known today as Wicca.[107] I count myself among the many witches who are part of the Gardnerian tradition, but the demand for Wicca, especially in the US, quickly outstripped the slow, teacher-to-student initiatory path. New traditions formed, mostly invented out of whole cloth and often influenced by whatever was available in print about Wicca. In the 1990s, "eclectic Wicca," of no tradition and requiring no teachers, emerged as the dominant force in the US Wiccan movement. Still, however free-form, eclectic, and do-it-yourself one's Wicca may be in the twenty-first century, some of its DNA is from Gardner.

Indeed, many Pagan traditions picked up a lot of ritual techniques, customs, and language from Wicca. Today there are many Pagan paths and witchcraft practices that have worked to excise that influence. Many "reconstructionist" Pagans make an effort to get to the nitty-gritty of our ancestral Paganism without resorting to the nineteenth- and twentieth-century romanticism that influenced Wicca, and many forms of witchcraft entirely eschew the religious and ritual aspects of Wicca and Paganism. Yet the ideas that Wicca disseminated from the 1950s through the beginning of the twenty-first century show up throughout the p-word world, even among those who have no direct experience of Wicca. The DNA is there.

Gardner was a part of the British occult community of the first half of the twentieth century, the members of which were all influenced by people, or trained in groups, already mentioned. Gardner was involved in Freemasonry, met and studied briefly with Aleister Crowley, and was an initiate of the O.T.O.[108] His writings bore the distinct influence of the Golden Dawn.[109]

A number of Gardnerians and others have thoroughly analyzed Gerald Gardner's published works and determined that the word *polarity* never

---

107. See Heselton, *Witchfather*.

108. Heselton, *Witchfather*, 342–51.

109. Heselton, *Witchfather*, 389 and 391, as well as Gardner, *Witchcraft Today*, 47, among others.

appears. Yet the concepts are certainly prevalent. The passage I find most striking is this one:

> Some of these [a witch's] powers…depend on the possibility of forming a sort of human battery, as it were, of combined human wills working together…
>
> …To form this battery of wills, male and female intelligences are necessary in couples. In practice these are usually husband and wife.[110]

This certainly appears to partake of Fortune's idea of gender polarity being necessary for any magical work, although the "husband and wife" implication is that it's intended to be sexual, which Gardner emphasizes (homophobically) by saying that "great love" develops when people do magic together, and therefore it should always be male to female, or female to male.[111]

But Gardner also recognized that people, and gods, contain two genders and two poles:

> [The god] is symbolized by the High Priestess, standing with her arms crossed to represent the skull and crossbones. The worshipper kisses her feet, saying a sort of prayer.[112]

During this prayer to the High Priestess, she opens out her arms to the Pentacle position. She then represents the goddess, or regeneration, signifying that the prayer is granted. "Thus she has been both God and Goddess, male and female, death and regeneration, one might say bisexual."[113] (Note that the meaning of *bisexual* in this quote is "having two sexes/genders" and doesn't refer to orientation.)

Gardner initiated Doreen Valiente into Wicca in 1953,[114] and his tradition thereby acquired one of the great poets of witchcraft. Valiente was

---

110. Gardner, *Witchcraft Today*, 28–29.

111. Gardner, *Witchcraft Today*, 69.

112. Gardner, *Witchcraft Today*, 80.

113. Gardner, *Witchcraft Today*, 80–81.

114. Valiente, *The Rebirth of Witchcraft*, 47.

heavily influenced by both Aleister Crowley and Dion Fortune. Fortune is referenced in just about everything Valiente wrote. Valiente not only read Crowley, but recognized where Gerald had added bits of Crowley's poetry to his own rituals.[115] From these earlier occultists, Valiente learned Kabbalah, magical correspondences, and polarity. Indeed, it is Valiente who first used the word *polarity* in print in relation to Wicca.[116]

Toward the end of her life though, Valiente began to see polarity differently:

> We can question whether it is absolutely necessary for a coven to be made up of both sexes. This is insisting upon a manifestation upon the physical plane of something which may be more important upon the inner planes.[117]

The development of polarity ideas as we have inherited them can be fairly said to have ended before Wicca—the early twentieth century gives us magical polarity more or less in the form we know it today. But many modern magical people aren't familiar with Western occultism or the Western Mystery Traditions. They are nonetheless influenced by them because of the DNA they inherited through Gerald Gardner and Wicca.

Our Historical Journey

The Golden Dawn transmitted ideas about polarity to Aleister Crowley and Dion Fortune, influential occultists who disseminated these ideas widely. These ideas, as published in the 1920s, '30s, and '40s, remained basically intact in their original form as they traveled to a variety of magical traditions and mystery cults and into Wicca.

The Golden Dawn gave us gender polarity as defined by magical roles: women as goddesses and priestesses and men as gods and priests. Crowley added sex magic, eroticism, and the symbolic *hieros gamos* to our ideas about polarity. From Dion Fortune we inherited the idea of gender balance, magical

---

115. Valiente, *The Rebirth of Witchcraft*, 54.

116. Valiente, *Witchcraft for Tomorrow*, 28.

117. Valiente, *The Rebirth of Witchcraft* 184–85.

partnership, and polarity based solely on the presence of gendered bodies: polar energy just *is* if a man and a woman are present.

When people today argue against ideas of polarity that are repressive and gender normative, they are largely arguing with the Golden Dawn, Dion Fortune, or Thelema, even if they've never heard of any of them.

But how did we get here? In the ancient world, dualism was not at first about gender at all; it was about God and humanity. Gender gets defined in a very particular way, but it isn't functionally essential to the philosophies that explore these ideas.

In alchemy, we find the original idea of polarity energy, and it is defined with gender labels, but alchemy never *embodies* polarity. Sulfur may be male and mercury female, but polarity never involves the distinct bodies of men and women; an alchemist's gender is never a part of the experiment.

Kabbalah begins the process of understanding that polarity and sexuality can combine, that the abstraction of the Pillars is also the embodiment of a man and his wife representing God and his Shekhinah.

Alchemy and Kabbalah, as well as Hermetic philosophy, all then influenced the Western Mystery Traditions, Theosophy, the Golden Dawn, Aleister Crowley, and Dion Fortune; but by that point, the cultural baggage of a misogynist West was deeply entwined in those ideas.

And here we are today.

Our Original Questions

I started my dive into history with some questions. Now that we've done some exploring, let's return to those questions and see where we've landed.

Where did the idea of polarity originate?

We found roots of polarity in the ancient world, in the dualism of Aristotle and Plato. Nonetheless, it seems clear that alchemy is the first place where we see spiritual and magical power derived from separating and combining the poles.

Does polarity magic originate in or derive from sex magic or sexual ritual (especially the *hieros gamos*)?

Surprisingly, the answer to this one is no. I fully expected the origins of polarity work to be bound up in these ancient rites of sex and marriage. This is what I was taught as a little baby occultist. When I first began researching this book, I asked other occultists what they knew of the history of polarity (it being such a vast, nearly infinite field), and sexual rites are where I was directed to look.

Yet polarity is simply not there. The *hieros gamos* is a rite of fertility, sovereignty, and renewal. It is a rite of invocation—bringing a goddess into the body of the priestess. There is nothing in the ancient material that talks about polarity in relation to Sumer, or Babylon, or the Celtic sovereignty rites.

As surprised as I was to learn this, I also find it freeing. If the sacred marriage is inextricably bound to polarity magic, then polarity magic has an inherently heterosexual and gender-normative aspect. Knowing that this is not the case opens up space for queer people to explore polarity work without feeling we're missing some essential component.

It's true that polarity *can* be mixed with sacred sex, but knowing that it's not a requirement is genuinely liberating.

If so, when and how did the sex get removed [from polarity magic]?

You can see from my original questions that my assumptions about where I was heading were wrong. The history was revelatory. Rather than sex getting removed from polarity, it turns out polarity was added to sex. This started with the Renaissance Kabbalists but remained a Jewish mystery until Thelema made it explicit and ritualized it.

How did the idea of gender polarity get so incredibly abstract? How did we go from male and female to sun and moon?

Before there was polarity magic, the ancient Hellenic philosophers were dividing the universe into its component parts. They were mighty chart-makers, assigning correspondences to everything. So this dualism, with male and female attributes of everything and anything, actually predates polarity as we understand it.

For polarity that corresponds to gender labels, we again have to turn to alchemy. For polarity that takes those labels seriously, as referring to embodied gender, the gender of humans and the presumed gender of deity, our source is Kabbalah.

How did any or all of this turn into the modern concept of magical partnership?

For this, we have to thank Dion Fortune. Although you can call any number of things "partnership," it is from Fortune that we derive the modern concept of an opposite-sex couple who may or may not be romantically involved, who work magic together for the purpose of embodying polarity by the mere fact of their gender.

Fortune was born in the Victorian era but was a child when Queen Victoria died. Nonetheless, I tend to think of her sensibilities as Victorian. Her books are astonishingly magical and insightful. They're *useful* books to read, as well as inspiring. They're also homophobic, gender essentialist, racist, and anti-Semitic. (I'm sure I'm leaving something out.) So understanding that something comes from Dion Fortune is helpful: we can find the power and also acknowledge the limitations.

And knowing all this, we can now move on to section 2 and actually explore polarity in ways both imaginative and practical.

Journal/Discussion Prompts

- How much is your own practice influenced by Crowley? By Fortune? By the grimoire tradition? Are there things in your practice that you don't know the source of but that might be from this period? How does that feel?

- Are principles from *The Kybalion* a part of your practice? What do you think of these principles?

- How does it feel to have explored the history of polarity? Does it change your thinking or feelings about this topic?

SECTION TWO
POLARITIES AND BINARIES

Section Two

Discovering Polarities

In section 1 we explored the "what is it" of polarity. We defined it, and we saw ways in which it is wrongheaded as well as ways in which it is powerful. We delved into history, we found an underlying queerness, and we didn't shy away from legitimate complaints about homophobia and gender essentialism. We explored all of this with journaling and/or discussion prompts.

Now what?

Section 2 is arguably the fun part. It's more practical, more experiential, and more here-and-now.

I've spent a lot of time meditating, thinking, discussing, and exploring, and I've come up with a half dozen polarities that I think are essential to the very nature of polarity. That is, from among the lists and lists of paired polarities, I was able to sort all of them under these six. In addition, each of these six has a unique quality that none of the other five have, so I have a sense that I've gotten at something essential in creating this list of six.

One of the things that I have found liberating about this analysis is that there are *so many* ways to explore polarity energy. We've seen that gender polarity has been used in oppressive ways in the occult. Some people might choose not to use gender polarity at all so as not to have to unpack the history of misogyny and homophobia that it can be bound up in. It's also true that some people just aren't interested in working with gender polarity, whether it's oppressive or not. For many nonbinary people, gender polarity doesn't make internal sense. But with an array of polarity energy forms available, gender can be set aside while still working polarity—often very traditionally. If you want to skip the gender polarity section entirely, there's still a lot of powerful magic here to explore.

Any sorting system has a certain amount of arbitrariness built in. Many of these polarities could be arranged differently, this categorized as that, or as the other, or as a subset of yet another. At the same time, almost all of them are very individual, and you or I or someone else could decide one or another is its own self and not part of any other list. We'll encounter this nuance in the next chapter: Is passive/active its own polarity or part of force/form? This is where it's great that we embrace nuance, and nonbinariness, and can accept "both/and" as an answer instead of insisting upon "either/or." These categories make sense to me, and creating them has helped me understand polarity itself, but to a certain extent they're just a device to allow me to organize my thoughts into nice, neat chapters. Appendix B charts all the polarities listed in this book so you can see them for yourself and play around with re-sorting them if you like.

For each of the polarities that follow, we'll start with a description and discussion. Other polarities that I think fall in this category are also discussed (or at least listed). For each polarity, we'll also explore what a "third" is and how it might manifest.

We'll then talk about polarities in ways meaningful to Pagans, Wiccans, and occultists of all stripes. What gods and goddesses are expressive of this polarity? How is this polarity seen in human self-expression and relationship? What ritual acts and magical tools express this polarity? Each chapter offers at least one ritual. There are also discussion/journaling prompts following each ritual.

A word about ritual: I think I'm a pretty good ritualist. I also think that in every book that includes rituals (I own many such books and have written a few), the ritual itself is usually the least important part. One of the true assets of occult and magical people is our creativity. Many of us are good, or very good, ritualists. Many of us have a gift of spontaneity or a gift of scripting, or both, in a ritual context. So a printed ritual, in this book or any other, is merely a jumping-off point for the creative reader.

As I said in the introduction, I'm primarily Wiccan. I've written and participated in rituals from several different magical and Pagan traditions, but my bent is unmistakable. Thus you may find Wiccan footprints in my rituals that don't suit your taste. That's okay. Just as polarity is individual, so is ritual, and using my offerings here as the seeds from which your own rituals will grow is ideal.

One more thing: In a book about polarity, it is inevitable that many of the rituals require two people (at a minimum). It's also true that many occultists are solitary practitioners. Ideally, you know other occultists to share these rituals with. Although we all contain all poles within us, occultists have known for centuries that the easiest way to experiment with polar energy is to have two participants, one manifesting each pole. The journaling prompts I provide are a great way for even a solo practitioner to get value from the rituals, but working with others is empowering, and I hope that is available to you.

Let's get started.

Chapter Seven

Force and Form

The terms *force* and *form* come from Kabbalah, referring, respectively, to Chokmah and Binah, the second and third sephirot. In my exploration of polarities, I have come to think of this as one of the *ur*-polarities, one of perhaps only two polarities that are at the core of the very concept of polarity. **Force/form is the original polarity of creation.**

Think of Dr. Frankenstein's monster. Frankenstein needed two things to create life: he needed the body that he constructed out of parts, and he needed the lightning that he channeled with his amazing machine. Without the *force*, the lightning, there's just a corpse; but without the *form*, the body, there's just…lightning—a storm and nothing more.

In chapter 1, I quoted Lynna Landstreet describing polarity as the creation of life: lightning striking the primordial waters. This is force and form. In creation, there is always force, energy, power, the enlivening and animating spark, and there is always form, a vessel, a shape, a way of taking that force and turning it into something.

In the West, we talk about this as seed and womb, which is to say we gender force and form via the analogy of conception and birth. Force is male, the sperm, the energy that bursts forth. Form is female, the womb, the shape that contains and defines the seed so that it can become life.

Interestingly, though, Eastern thought takes the opposite approach. In Tantra, energy and power are female, as embodied by the goddess Shakti (sometimes spelled Sakti). Form and creation are male, as embodied by the god Shiva (sometimes spelled Siva and also known as Shakta or Sakta). Shiva's power is Shakti, and that which he manifests depends on her power. To quote Sanskrit scholar Sir John Woodroffe:

> S'iva [is] the name for the changeless aspect of the One whose power of action and activity is S'akti....
>   ...Every Hindu believes in S'akti as God's Power."[118]

If you are accustomed to the Western magical system, it could seem like a biological imperative that the womb is form, which is impregnated with seed/force. The feminine as the activator may seem counterintuitive. One is tempted indeed to understand womb/female as *fact*. But the difference between East and West here can awaken us to the power of changing perceptions. It's not just that we are made aware that our understanding of binary polarity is cultural; it's that both systems *work*. Because our internal polar circuits are complex and not tied to any one set of facts, biology, or culture, we can choose to understand polarity in complex ways. Any of us is capable of working a Western magical system and choosing to embody a womb/seed metaphor, thereby deriving enormous power. We are also equally capable of embodying Shiva/Shakti, switching the force/form polarity and still deriving enormous power. This is true heterosexually and it is also true with any two people of any gender and orientation.

We can return to electrons and protons, electrons moving toward, protons staying still, so that electrons are force and protons are form. It's interesting how often Western sources fall back to electricity as a metaphor for gender polarity, with "negative" defined as female, yet here it's the "male" protons that await the action of the "female." It is electrons, rushing forward, that are force, while protons, holding and absorbing their force, correspond to form.

Because we can see form as holding still and force as moving toward form, we can correspond this polarity to passive (form) and active (force).

---

118. Woodroffe, *S'akti and S'ākta*, 18.

Let's set that aside though and deal with passive and active as a separate polarity. One way we can talk about the distinction is that force/form is a more cosmic polarity and passive/active is more earthly.

Force without form is undifferentiated energy. It can be wasted, dissipated energy that goes nowhere, an excessively hyperactive kid bouncing off the walls and accomplishing nothing, or it can be the negative side of uncontained energy: violence. Form without force is unmoving, dead matter.

The Third

Force and form combined is the polarity of creation. It is the Big Bang: a stable core (form) moving outward (force) to become a universe (the created third). Again returning to Landstreet's beautiful imagery, a spark (force) strikes a lifeless ocean (form) and the first life forms emerge.

This *is* life, which is why force-form is, to me, a crucial and life-affirming polarity, one that is as meaningful to the queerest enby as to the most heteronormative person on the planet.

The third for force-form is possibility, inspiration, new creation, and regeneration. Force and form are the beginning, and emergence itself is the third.

Other Polarities That Are Force/Form

One of the ways I came up with all these various polarities was just by discussing it with people on social media. From interesting and often wide-ranging conversations with other occultists, I culled a sizable list. Both **matter/energy** and **matter/spirit** came up in these discussions.

These are so close to what we've already described about force/form that they're almost not another polarity so much as a paraphrase. However, there's a touch of nuance here: matter/spirit takes us back to Plato and to the *Hermetica*, with matter being the "false" and spirit being the "true." When seen in this way, as being in opposition rather than as interacting in a complementary manner, it's dualism—a "good" and "bad" is implied. More truly *polar* are matter and energy. Matter is the earth, the womb, the creator, receiving energy, which is the lightning, the seed, the inspiration. Energy is the animating force, and matter is that which is animated. Animation itself is the third.

Physical and agricultural polarities abound, including **seed/vessel** and **field/plow.** Here, the seed and the plow introduce energy/fertility/movement/force into the vessel or field, which is a static and unmoving form that contains seed or is changed by plow. These concepts are commonplace and accessible.

The manifestation of force and form can be seen as a polarity between **time** and **space.** Space can easily be understood as corresponding to form. Both are the "is" of manifest reality; form and space are where we keep all the things. But force and time don't necessarily seem like part of the same thing until we see both as, well, the thing that isn't space. With both force and time, movement is unconstrained by space/form. Force acts upon form, shaping it and awakening it, as time acts upon space, eroding land, moving shorelines, shifting continents. The late Alexei Kondratiev, a scholar of Celtic paganism and folklore, used to say that the Goddess was geography, while the God was history. First, we have to understand that "Goddess" here means form, as in Mother Nature, and "God" means force. (This is the same principle by which *The Kybalion* divided divinity into Mother/Nature and Father/God.) **History/geography** directly parallels time/space—history moves and changes and it brings the possibility of the unknown, while geography is static, stable, and incontrovertible.

Finally, we can understand **fate/choice** as a polarity or tension that directly corresponds to geography (the body that stands still) and history (the changes wrought by action).

Deities of Force and Form

In the Kabbalah, force is **Chokmah,** and form is **Binah.** Sephirot are not deities, but the many planetary and deity (and other) correspondences for Kabbalah make the Kabbalistic stuff valuable for constructing ritual and making spiritual connections through these polarities. For that reason, I'll include Kabbalistic correspondences for all polarities from here on out. If you want to see how all these polarities map onto the Tree of Life, see appendix A.

In *The Sea Priestess*, Dion Fortune implicitly makes this connection when she ties Binah into a song of a supernal goddess of Form:

> "I am she who ere the earth was formed
>   Was Ea, Binah, Ge
> I am that soundless, boundless, bitter sea,
> Out of whose deeps life wells eternally."[119]

With *Ge*, Fortune is making a rhyme for *sea* out of **Gaia**. She is earth/form and partnered with **Chronus**/time.

A lot of traditional pairs of earth/sky work here, especially at the cosmic/creation level. **Rhea/Uranus** convey the same meaning as Gaia/Chronus.

It's unclear who Fortune meant by "Ea," since she is invoking the Goddess (her ritual is strictly duotheistic) and Ea is a name for the Mesopotamian god Enki. For a Mesopotamian pairing, **Apsu** is the god of the sweet waters, and **Tiamat** the goddess of the salt water (Fortune's "bitter sea"). Tiamat is considered chief here, the mother of all and ruler of creation, but both she and her husband, Apsu, are primordial. They are killed by the younger gods, who want control over their own fate, led by **Marduk.**

Many primordial pairings speak of the earth before some crucial creation event: earth is form without force, then encountered by force so that humankind is born. With Rhea/Uranus, this "encounter" is sexual, while with Tiamat/Marduk, it is murderous.

Force and Form in Humanity

The polarity of force and form is a necessary one for human wellbeing, and it is a place in which we cannot and should not rely on our relationships, but should work to build an inner circuit that we can know and experience.

---

119. Fortune, *The Sea Priestess*, 190.

It's certainly true that this polarity can be made manifest in relationships. To the extent that seed/womb is treated literally, you generally need the partner, at least for a few minutes. But if we look at what these qualities represent in a human life, they are so expansive and so essential that confining them to making babies seems to me to very much miss the point.

Force without form is violence, chaos, randomness, and the ceaseless movement that produces nothing. It's the next good idea, and the next one, and the next one, but nothing gets done. There's no shape to these ideas, no manifestation. By contrast, form without force is stagnation. It is sitting still endlessly. It's the fear of change. Disorders like agoraphobia and compulsive hoarding are related to this attachment to space without movement.

Force can bring *just do it* energy to form; paradoxically, form can bring *just do it* manifestation to force—"do it" meaning either pull forth some *inner* energy *or* give some shape to this energy. They say "where there's a will, there's a way." Force is the will and form is the way. In a relationship, this can be the supportiveness of having the right push to give to your friend or partner at the right moment.[120]

In a partnership, it can often be true that when one partner is deeply engaged in creating change, the other partner can best contribute by creating space. If you're a political or military spouse keeping the home fires burning while your partner is doing transformative work, that is a force/ form relationship. The politician is manifesting history, while the partner on the apparent back burner is manifesting geography. There's no need, in such a relationship, for the force/form energies to be permanently locked in place. When a woman puts her wife through college, she is form while her wife is force; the college graduate can then enter the workforce and become the supportive "form" spouse, allowing her wife to manifest force by going through school in turn.

---

120. By "relationship," I mean any human relationship, whether friend, lover, spouse, coworker, parent/child, sibling, etc. I'll generally just say "partner" throughout, and I'll generally imply that there are exactly two partners. Your mileage may vary.

Magical Tools of Force and Form

Any projective tool that communicates or embodies outward movement is a tool of force, including the sword, athame, wand, and staff. Any tool that holds, contains, or shapes is a tool of form, including the cup, pentacle, and cauldron. The symbolic Great Rite discussed in chapter 3 is a ritual of force and form.

In 777, Crowley corresponds Chokmah, force, with the "Lingam" (phallus) and the "Inner Robe of Glory." Binah is the "Yoni" and the "Outer Robe of Concealment."[121] I think it's interesting that the phallus, an external organ, is equated with an "inner" robe, and the yoni, which is decidedly concave, is the "outer." It definitely reads to me like these tools are a kind of both/and polarity—the phallus going from outer to inner, and the yoni going from inner to outer. (Yoni and Lingam as tools are probably meant to describe the sacred Hindu objects—usually a single object combining both—representing Shakti and Shiva.)

As a young occultist, I was taught that 777 was an essential source for correspondences. I find some of the correspondences helpful, some of them confusing, and some of them outmoded, but I am including them precisely because they were once essential occult knowledge, and so they can provide illumination if not for current work, then at least for the occult underpinnings of our understanding of polarity.

Force and Form in Ritual

Many magical traditions that divide roles by gender are *de facto* dividing by the poles of force and form. Standing as it does at the top of the Tree of Life, this polarity is seen as flowing down into and through all magical ritual.

In traditional Wicca, there have long been complaints that men are treated like "glorified altar boys."[122] In fact, what is happening is that there are rituals in which men are embodying force and women are embodying

---

121. Crowley, 777, page 13 of *Book Two*.
122. Bonewits, "Pagan Men, Unite!"

form. Once we understand this, we can unhook the gender dynamic and ask what is actually occurring.

Dividing gender roles along force/form lines goes back to the earliest days of Wicca. Doreen Valiente, who worked with Gerald Gardner as a high priestess, specifically compared Chokmah and Binah to the role of the priest and priestess in Wicca. Chokmah, she said, was the "archetypal masculine" and Binah, the "archetypal feminine," but once you look past the idea that a symbolic gender label is the same as human gender, you can see force and form permeating Wiccan ritual—and once you see that, you see that the human gender is not the key part at all, something we already noted that Valiente herself came to understand later in life. In the same passage quoted, Valiente goes on to say, "They actually represent that fundamental and divine polarity which underlies all manifested nature, the two opposites whose union constitutes the symbolical Great Work of alchemy."[123]

As with any ritual, a couple working a force/form polarity should explicitly understand and agree to this dynamic.[124] Since the "force" part can be less showy, it's not a great role for a theatrical person who enjoys acting out ritual drama. Certainly, though, there's room for adding a ritual step to build force into that person with plenty of flair.

The Force/Form Ritual

Force/form polarity can be used to empower almost any ritual you already do. Choose a ritual that is comfortable and familiar and add this dynamic to it, or replace an existing "partnership" dynamic with this one to see how it feels.

Force/Form: Begin by holding hands and/or holding eye contact.

Force: Focus on giving Form power. Imagine yourself as an open spigot of energy, directed at your partner. Visualize your partner as a deity of form and yourself as a worshiper.

---

123. Valiente, *Witchcraft for Tomorrow*, 28.

124. By "couple," I mean two people, not any particular flavor of couple.

Form: Focus on receiving power. Visualize your partner as powerful and as trustworthy. Allow yourself to be open and receptive to being empowered and animated by your partner. Visualize your partner as a deity of force and yourself as a worshiper.

If there is a group present, all raise power through your usual means (dance, drumming, breath work, toning, etc.) and send it into Force for their use in the ritual.

Now, for all subsequent ritual steps, Form performs the step while Force sends power into Form. Whenever Form is to use a magical tool, Force picks it up, mentally sends power into it, and hands it to Form.

Example: A Wiccan Circle-Casting

Force: *I am Force and you are Form. I am Chokmah and you are Binah. I give all my power to you for use in creation. So mote it be!* (Exchange a kiss.)

Form: *I am Form and you are Force. I am Binah and you are Chokmah. I accept your power, I take it into me. I shape it, and with it I shape worlds. I blend you with me to create this ritual, I blend you with me to create power. So mote it be!* (Exchange a kiss.)

Force: (Lifts sword) *Power of the sword, power of Air, power to cast, to direct, to shape, and to form, be present.*

(Hands sword to Form.)

Form: (Spoken while circumambulating the circle, east to east, with the sword) *I conjure here the circle of power, that it be a meeting place of joy and love, that it be a shield and protection, that it be a universe and a nest, a safe space and a space of possibility. Circle, be bound, be guarded, be consecrated. In the names of [gods being worshiped], so mote it be!*

Force: (Silently sends power into Form throughout.)

Form: (Returns to the altar.)

Force: (Lifts the dish of salt water, sending power into it through their hands, then hands the dish to Form.)

Form: (Again circumambulating, sprinkling the circle) *By Water and Earth, I cleanse this circle. By love and strength, it is cleansed.*

Force: (Silently sends power into Form throughout.)

Force: (Lifts the censer of incense, sending power into it through their hands, then hands the censer to Form.)

Form: (Again circumambulating, censing the circle) *By Fire and Air, I bless this circle. By power and intelligence, it is blessed.*

Force: (Silently sends power into Form throughout.)

The circle is now cast. The entire ritual continues in this manner.

Journal/Discussion Prompts

- How does the force/form dynamic change your understanding of ritual steps already familiar to you?
- How does a shift from "magical partnership" to "force and form" feel?
- Do you experience a relationship between force/form and gender?
- Are you comfortable with language about "archetypal" feminine and masculine? Is language about Chokmah and Binah more comfortable? Force and form?
- Do you have a preference for one role over the other?

Chapter Eight

Self and Other

If force/form is the *ur*-polarity of creation, then self/other is the *ur*-polarity of perception. It's the first perception that leads to the very idea of polarity: the knowledge that there *is* self and other is how we begin to explore the energies of interacting between poles. If I am all there is, then there are no poles. If other is all there is, then I am alone, and again, there is no polarity. Only when I perceive the truth of the energy exchange known as self and other does polarity have meaning.

Self and other is the *ur*-polarity of consciousness and of philosophy. It's the beginning of how we understand our place in the universe. We perceive that there is an other, that we are both alone and not alone. This is an inherently polar energy: We seek toward and we pull back; we merge and fail to merge. Self and other is a space of longing.

In a sense, self/other is all self. It is the self that perceives itself and perceives that there is an other. Paradoxically, other is as much defined by self as self is. Other, after all, is that which is not me, just as self is that which *is* me.

Historically, this is where ideas about both dualism and polarity begin. As we've discussed, polarity begins not as male/female but as divine/human, which is kind of the ultimate us/them. That which I understand and that which is beyond me. Ordinary versus *whoa*.

Part of self/other is the split between mind/body, which we saw in our earlier discussion of dualism. This is Plato's dualism: the body is "false"; it's "just flesh." What it really is, when we experience this particular dualism, is a prison. I cannot touch the mind/soul/being of another (whether human or divine) because my body is an impenetrable barrier.

The Third

For self/other, the third is oneness, transcendence, merging. I think this polarity is one of the places where sex magic (or just sex) really comes in, and in a completely nongendered way. For most people, sex is one of the ways to transcend the mind/body split. We use the body to transcend the body. If we are lucky, we've experienced that moment of sexual oneness, where we are one with our partner, where the barrier between you and me is completely dissolved.

I've been in that space. I've had visions, I've seen stars, I've *tripped out* in that space. One is inclined to say it's love, but that's not accurate. It *might* be—you might have that experience with a beloved. I'd wager it's hard to have that experience *without* the trust and openness present with a beloved. Yet it's not love that takes you there. Rather, it's the experience of stepping outside one's bodily limitations. Extreme pleasure, purely intense physical sensation, combined with a trusting ability to let go to that sensation, as well as a willingness to merge with that particular other (hence usually beloved) are the ingredients. When that happens and the stars are aligned, the divide between self and other ends for a moment, and that moment can change everything.

We'll talk more about sex magic in section 3. For now, it's enough to understand that physical pleasure and trust are not gendered experiences. You can experience this with a partner of any sex, and you can experience this with more than one partner.

I don't wish to exclude asexual people. Sex isn't the only way to experience transcendence. It's honestly the way I know best, and for people who are sexual, it's often the easiest. Religious ecstasy and deep trance are similarly transcendent, and some "mob" experiences are as well. There are times that concert attendees can be transported by the music and the divide between themselves, the musicians, and the other attendees can dissolve into a sea of musical joy. Mob mentality, dangerous as it can be, is the transcendent experience of being one with a group and losing one's individuality in that group. Mobs are dangerous exactly because transcendence is so enticing.

Sensory flooding or its opposite is usually necessary to create the transcendent experience: silent meditation, physical austerity, sexual sensation, the noise and overstimulation of a crowd.

Transcendence is the liminal state between self and other. The mediating state that is a "third" of self/other is community. Community can also be seen as the creative product of self/other. It's what happens when we choose to engage with this polarity to create meaning.

Community—human interconnection—works best when we understand it as an engagement with this polarity. By contrast, community tends to break down when we forget this polarity. When we think "everyone here is like me" or "everyone here agrees with me" or "everyone here thinks like me," then we are forgetting that there's a polarity at work, that other is essentially unknowable, and that community is meant to overcome differences and mediate distance and not just be easy.

Other Polarities That Are Self/Other

We've already touched upon one of the core polarities experienced as self/other: **humanity/divinity.** This is the polar tension that leads us to religious experience, to seeking the third of transcendence. Similarly, the polarity of **lover/beloved** leads us to seek sexual or romantic transcendence. Religious or mystical experience is the seeking of a third between self/other as divine/human, and romantic love is the seeking of a third between self/other as lover/beloved.

Returning to the experience of the divine, we find the polarity of **transcendence** and **immanence.** This is a different meaning entirely of the word *transcendence.* It often isn't seen as a polarity at all, but as a theology or point of view. In this sense, transcendent deity is deity outside oneself;

a unique and separate being. Jesus Christ is a transcendent deity in traditional Christianity. You are not Christ; Christ might be within you, but he is not you. By contrast, immanent deity is deity that is within; you may understand that deity as having a distinct identity but also as being entirely within the self (hence a self/other connection).

I see transcendent/immanent deity as a polarity, because the truth is we don't really know whether the gods are within us, apart from us, or both. The nature of deity may be a philosophical system or an opinion, but it's not objectively knowable. Therefore, in our spiritual and mystical lives, we are experiencing an energetic interplay of deity is me/deity is other. We are flowing back and forth along a polarity of *where* I experience spiritual connection.

Expansion/contraction is perhaps not obvious at first. Hippies introduced the term *consciousness expansion*, but remember that in polarities, we understand terms to be relative. If something is expanded, it is relative to something more contracted. Consciousness expansion assumes the mind is in a contracted state, limited, cut off, not touching that which is beyond its contracted reach. Through drugs, meditation, or other experiences, you expand your mind beyond its boundaries. In an expanded state, we find oneness with other beings because as we break down walls (which are contracted), we find the truth of our overlapping and mutually connected selves. The *Lazy Man's Guide to Enlightenment* tells us:

> The basic function of each being is expanding and contracting. Expanded beings are permeative; contracted beings are dense and impermeative....
>
> A completely expanded being is space. Since expansion is permeative, we can be in the "same space" with one or more other expanded beings....
>
> [...]

...To the degree that he is contracted, a being is unable to be in the same space with others, so contraction is felt as fear, pain, unconsciousness, ignorance, hatred, evil.[125]

Notice the slip into dualism: contraction is equated with evil and is the thing to be avoided. The consciousness expansion movement definitely didn't want us to be contracted. But now let's look at it in a more polar way: to be contracted is to be entirely self, to be expanded is to be entirely other, and as the energy moves, breathing in and out, we shift between states of more or less isolated as self, more or less interconnected as other. As a visual and tangible metaphor, it allows for exploration of the polarity in a different way.

Compare expansion/contraction to *solve et coagula* (dissolve and conjoin) as described in chapter 5. The alchemical process dissolves (expands) the self or a substance into component parts and then reunites (contracts) them. But here contraction is integration and healing. These contrasting expressions of polarity show us that it's not about which pole is "good" but about energy movement between the poles.

Lover/beloved is a particular (and beautiful) subset of **subject/object.** If you haven't explored this idea philosophically or spiritually, you may have heard of it socially or politically, especially if you've heard a woman complain about being "objectified" by men. What does this mean?

To be objectified is to be treated as an object. It can be a good, beloved, praised object, or it can be an ignored object, or it can be a hated object. The core truth of an object is that it has no external agency and can only be acted upon or experienced by the subject. An object is assumed to have no inner experience.

If I walk around an obstacle on the sidewalk, it is merely an object and I don't concern myself with how it feels about being avoided. If I gaze admiringly at a painting in a museum, I don't consider how the painting feels about being stared at, admired, or loved. I am the subject, I am the

---

125. Golas, *The Lazy Man's Guide to Enlightenment*, 13–15. This little book had a cult following in the 1970s. It's very dated.

author of my experience, and I am the one with choices—to avoid or not, to admire or not. Only my point of view has meaning.

In the classic feminist example, a man whistles at or catcalls a woman on the street. The man then says, "What's the problem? It was a compliment." The problem, of course, is the woman is an object. The man really doesn't care if the woman enjoys the compliment (as evidenced by the fact that her objection is dismissed as unimportant). As far as he's concerned, only his inner experience matters, because he's the only subject. When such a man says he "doesn't understand women," he's saying he doesn't understand how *objects* are the subjects of their own lives and the authors of their own experience.

Subject/object, when understood as a polarity, means there's an energy exchange as we objectify one another and also give energy to the other's subjective experience. When I admire Professor Spouse's body, I am objectifying her (sometimes in a really vulgar way, to be honest), and then I let go of that and give her the ability to have a subjective experience: yes, admire my butt, or no, I don't feel comfortable with that right now. Then I take that energy back from her and incorporate it into my own subjective experience. When subject/object is a polarity, no one is diminished.

Recently I was discussing polarity with my friend Maggi, and they mentioned getting great power out of the center/circumference polarity. This was one I'd never thought about, but as we talked and as I thought about it later, I found it very powerful. I'm going to reserve center/circumference for a later chapter and talk about the very similar concept of **planet/satellite:** that which is at the center, and that which is on the outside, circling it.

The energy being explored in planet/satellite is an energy of focus. The first thing you might think is that *self* is cognate with *planet*. After all, my self, my ego, is the center of my being. I think of the movie *About a Boy*, in which the lead character, Will (played by Hugh Grant), says, "The thing is, a person's life is like a TV show. I was the star of *The Will Show*. And *The Will Show* wasn't an ensemble drama. Guests came and went, but I was the regular. It came down to me and me alone."[126] He's saying (hilariously) that Will is the planet, and all the other people in his life were merely satellites.

But the energy of focus is not necessarily the energy of egoism. We can see that in the polarity of lover/beloved, the lover focuses and the beloved is the focus. Thus, the lover can be seen as a satellite orbiting the beloved.

On November 19, 2020, news host Rachel Maddow discussed on air how her life partner, Susan Mikula, had been very sick with COVID-19 and how terrifying the experience had been. She said, in part:

> If you know me personally at all, then the foremost thing you probably know about me is that I am in love....It was love at first sight.
>
> That has never waned....
>
> [...]
>
> ...Susan really is the center of my universe. And the way that I think about it is not that she is the sun and I'm a planet that orbits her....
>
> ...I think of it as a much more pitiful thing, that she is the planet and I am a satellite, and I'm up there sort of beep, beep, beeping at her and blinking my lights and trying to make her happy.
>
> ...I'm one of the lucky people on this earth....She's the organizing principle of my life.[127]

The energy of planet and satellite is not necessarily that of romance, although Maddow's declaration of love stands with Sappho or Shakespeare for its poetry and beauty. But the idea of the planet as an organizing principle, and the satellite as that which is organized, is truly a stunning way of exploring polar energy. Here I think of the third as the orbit itself, because without a planet, a satellite just shoots off into space. The third is gravitation.

---

126. IMDb, "About a Boy (2002): Hugh Grant: Will Freeman."

127. MSNBC, "Transcript: The Rachel Maddow Show, November 19, 2020." As of this writing, Susan is fully recovered and healthy.

Deities of Self and Other

One of the ways that self/other can be seen in deities is to work with the most distant gods. In many mythologies, a deity creates the world and then recedes, leaving other gods to run things. **Brahma** is the Hindu creator from whom other gods emerge. **Ahura Mazda,** the Wise Lord of Zoroastrianism, is similar—distant, powerful, and utterly other. In looking at such deities (there are quite a few of this nature), we don't correspond them to a deity of self, but rather we humans are self and deity is other.

Another approach is to look at gods and heroes who tried to mediate the distance between self and other, between gods and humanity. Take, for example, **Icarus.** In Greek myth, **Helios** is the sun, **Daedalus** is the human inventor who created wings but knew to avoid flying too close to Helios, and Icarus is Daedalus's son, who failed to heed his father's advice. When Icarus flew too close to the sun, the wax that affixed his wings melted, and he fell to his death. In this triad, Icarus is the self pole and Helios is the other, while Daedalus mediates the space between, finding a way to move between poles without destroying himself.

Another mediating being is **Atlas,** a Titan of Greek mythology. When the Titans lost their war with the Olympians, Atlas was punished by being made to stand at the edge of the world and hold up the sky. As a being who stands between humankind and the gods, and holds the space between them, Atlas is a force of movement between the poles of self and other.

In Kabbalah, we can see **Hod** and **Netzach** as self and other. Hod (Glory), the eighth sephirah, is self and corresponds to **Mercury,** while Netzach (Victory) is other and corresponds to **Venus.** Hod is also beneath Binah on the left pillar and carries energy of form, while Netzach is beneath Chokmah on the right pillar and carries energy of force. In this way, Netzach is the impulse (force) toward connection, while Hod is the act of connection—Hod gives it form. Together, their energy flows back and forth along the self/other pole.

My meditations also brought me to the idea that this pole is expressed between **Malkut** (Kingdom/self) and **Keter** (Crown/other). Because Malkut is the world in which we live, it represents the body and humanity. Keter is the highest we can get on the Tree of Life, the closest to the ultimate supernal nature of God. I had a rather interesting conversation about this with my friend Jack Chanek, when he questioned why I would include Malkut/Keter as a pairing in this section:

Me: Malkut is the world, the limitations of the body. Keter is the transcendent godhead.

Jack: Does that make Keter the other though? Freedom from the limitations of the body doesn't immediately strike me as being the same thing.

Me: Yes, because one of the cognate polarities is humans/gods. I'm seeing self/other as the source of dualism, which is human/God. That's a direct correspondence to me.

Jack: The reason I'm hesitant is that I feel like self/other is rooted in differentiation. I am me and you are you, and those are two separate things. But I feel like Keter doesn't perceive differentiation. I am Keter and you are Keter, and there's no point in talking about me or you because we're all just Keter.

Me: Interesting. In creation, Keter precedes the existence of humanity. So I think of it that way, as oneness preceding creation.

Jack: Sure, I can see that.

Me: Now I have to meditate on a Keter that's here and now, not just primordial.[128]

So that was fun.

Another way of looking at this Kabbalistic angle is that Netzach/Hod is self/other as mediated by community, while Keter/Malkut is self/other as mediated by transcendence. Of course, Netzach, being Venus, is very

---

128. WhatsApp chat with Jack Chanek, September 2, 2021. Chanek is the author of *Qabalah for Wiccans*.

sexual, so Netzach/Hod is also mediated by sex, which carries transcendent energy.

Ultimately, Keter/Malkut as a polarity has a deeper correspondence to our next polarity (passive/active), so for tidiness, it can be eliminated from this chapter. However, if it enhances your meditations and explorations, go for it.

Self and Other in Humanity

This section may seem out of place when discussing self/other since a corresponding pole to self *is* humanity. However, there's plenty of room to set aside the divine/human differentiation and discuss the self/other polarity as it exists between and among humans.

We've already touched on this: self and other is lover/beloved and subject/object. How does this manifest in our lives?

The Manic Pixie Dream Girl (a term coined by film critic Nathan Rabin) is an example of an idealized woman who exists in a cis male writer's imagination.[129] She is neither a Doris Day/"good girl" type nor a *femme fatale*. Instead, she's delightful, quirky, fun-loving, and just aggressive enough to shake up a sad and repressed male protagonist. What makes any of these "types" merely a type is that they have no interior life. They exist only from the point of view of the protagonist. A different film trope, discussed at length by filmmaker Spike Lee, is the "Magical Negro."[130] Again, this is a character (in this case African-American) who exists solely to help a white person or otherwise move a white person's plot forward. Manic Pixie Dream Girls, femmes fatale, and Magical Negros are all examples of "othering."[131]

Othering is when a group (women and African-Americans in the examples here, but it could be disabled people, or immigrants, or fat people,

---

129. Rabin, "The Bataan Death March of Whimsy Case File #1: *Elizabethtown*."

130. For example, Seitz, "The Offensive Movie Cliche That Won't Die."

131. Merriam-Webster, "Can 'Other' Be Used as a Verb?"

or queer people, etc.) is treated as alien.[132] As we discussed with objectification, it really doesn't matter if the "other" is liked or disliked. After all, protagonists fall in love with the Manic Pixie Dream Girl, and she changes their lives for the better. What matters here is that other is object; other is dehumanized. As a plot device, what we see most is the lack of interiority—characters who exist without an inner life, because only the white, able-bodied, straight, male (etc.) characters have that. In real life, it's more destructive and more insidious. It is the root of bigotries of all types. Othering speaks to a default human: In print, you'll often see that there are disabled people, or Asian people, or fat people without a corresponding observation that there are able-bodied, white, or thin people. The "default person" need not be called out by category, because we just assume that's what "person" means. So while a newspaper article might use the wording "Joe Smith, who uses a wheelchair," you will not typically see "Joe Smith, who is able-bodied."

When we are the ones being othered, it is not just infuriating, it's disorienting. I know I'm self, but I'm being treated as other; it feels like being displaced. This sense of isolation leads to higher levels of depression in marginalized groups. It turns out, for example, that bisexuals are more depressed than either straight or gay people, apparently because we are othered by both groups.[133]

We started out by discussing that self/other is a polarity generated within the self. Other exists because the self observes that something is not itself. In society and human relations writ large, we see how dehumanizing and dangerous that is. Othering, in society, is each individual self committing to its position, to its self-perception, to being "contracted" rather

---

132. I use the word *fat* in the sense of fat positivity. As a fat person, I've found great power in reclaiming this word and removing the stigma from it. *Fat* is factual and objective, and I don't want to shy from it. *Overweight*, by contrast, assumes an ideal weight that one can be over (or under). Other words I could use instead of *fat* (like *curvy* or *full-bodied*) tend to be euphemistic, as though being fat is so offensive you can't even say it. I know the word can make many people uncomfortable, so I hope you can read it in the positive spirit in which it's intended.

133. Neal, "A New Study Shows Why Bisexual People May Have Higher Rates of Depression."

than "expanded." It is seeing opposition and duality in difference, instead of polarity. Saying "we're all one" or "differences don't matter," no matter how well-meaning, is also a kind of erasure; it is ignoring polarity. "This isn't really polar" doesn't actually do anything toward connecting the poles. Connection happens through acknowledgment of differences and celebrating them—electrons racing toward protons rather than being repelled.

In individual relationships, othering plays out in the myriad ways in which we can fail to see our partner as fully human. Allowing myself to perceive this polarity brings the knowledge that I will never live inside any head but my own and that the inner thoughts of my beloved will always be a mystery to some extent. This is a painful truth of our existence, and we want badly to make that pain go away. This can lead to objectification: my beloved is always "my beloved" and never a lover in her own right.

It has been a profound thing, in my marriage, to sometimes stop seeing my spouse as my beloved and instead look at myself as *her* beloved. We naturally tend to measure our relationships by how they feel to us. What are my needs and are they being met? What do I wish my partner would do, and is she up to the task? But I can switch up the script when I look at her as lover and myself as beloved—her as subject and myself as object. Only from that perspective can I truly observe the effort she makes to figure out what my needs are and how to meet them. Once I see that, then even if my needs aren't always met, I see the thoughtfulness and consideration in a new light, and it is moving. It is expansive.

Another way of seeing self/other in human relationships is in the forming of communities, as already discussed. Humans want and need community. Even the most introverted among us grows unhappy if they're alone all the time. Likewise, even the most extroverted will lose their minds a little if they don't get a little alone time. A balance between social and solitude is needed, moving those electrons back and forth.

Self without other can be narcissism, egomania, vanity, and a host of negative traits. Other without self in an individual is, basically, a doormat, a self-sacrificing person who puts themselves last and suffers for it. Self balanced by other reduces egomania to a manageable size—to self-worth and earned pride. Other balanced by self becomes compassion, kindness, and generosity without being self-destructive.

Magical Tools of Self and Other

The magical tools that mediate the space between self and other can be the tools of sharing and community. The plate and the cauldron: these are tools of mutuality.

A mirror is a tool that can be used to explore the self part of self/other. In addition, a black mirror is a traditional tool of scrying. With this tool we can both see ourselves and "see" others, or other parts of reality.

An idol and an offering bowl as a paired set are tools that hold the space between divinity and humanity. Since ritual space is where the divine and human meet, that space (a circle for Wiccans, for example) can be seen as such a tool as well, as can the altar.

Crowley's 777 gives the "Lamp and Girdle" for Netzach and "the Names and Versicles and Apron" as Hod (none of which I find particularly useful, but your mileage may vary).

Self and Other in Ritual

To a certain extent, ritual itself is (or can be) a polarity rite of self/other as we juxtapose and attempt to traverse the space between humans and the divine. As with any polarity, this underlying current can be made explicit in order to more deeply explore the energy and power of that polarity.

Rituals of community are self/other rituals, as they create and sanctify the meditating third of this polarity. Any ritual that brings someone into a community is a ritual of self/other, so an initiation or dedication, in which a person enters the ritual space as an individual but leaves as a part of a greater whole, is flowing between the self/other poles.

Self/Other Ritual

Although a self/other ritual could be devised for use by two people (partners) or indeed by a solitary person (with self being the person and other being the divine, or ancestors, or an absent party), I thought it would be interesting to create a group ritual for this polarity. Especially since we always envision and ritualize polarity as "two," here's an opportunity to instead explore polarity energy flowing from one to many and back again. I've done variations on the following ritual several times, and despite its simplicity, it is surprisingly powerful.

Form ritual space in your usual manner, placing the self/other rite into the spot normally reserved for "work," or just get together and ground and center so that you are ready for ritual work to begin. It is helpful to review the steps of the ritual in advance, so everyone knows what's expected of them.

The steps denote a "leader," which just means the person who is scripted to move the ritual from step to step and doesn't require a leadership position in the group if you don't normally have that.

The ritual assumes that the group has a name. If you don't have one, choose a name or designation for the occasion.

The Self/Other Circle

The group stands in a circle.

Leader: *Self and other. Apart and together. Alone and loved. Allow this polarity to flow in your mind. Take a deep breath and notice yourself. Notice that you are one person. As you breathe, notice that there are others here. It is beautiful to be connected to them. Allow yourself to feel the desire for connection.*

One by one, we shall step forward and declare ourselves as Self. (The leader can go first so that everyone is reminded of how this is to be done.)

First Person: (Steps to center) *I am [name]. I am [short description].* (Example: *I am Deborah. I am a writer.*)

Everyone: (Repeats the name. Example: *Deborah. Deborah. Deborah.* This can be done a set number of times or just allowed to rise and fall naturally. It should be pretty brief, consistent with the feeling of an isolated Self. Then the first person steps back into place.)

Each person: (Steps to center) *I am [name]. I am [short description].*

Everyone: (Repeats the name as before. Then the person steps back. This continues until everyone has been in the center.)

Leader: (Takes the hands of the people on either side of them—this is the universal signal for everyone to join hands, and it always works. Then the leader repeats each name once. For example: *Deborah. Joe. Tate. Willow. Skylark.*)

We are more than self. We are a whole greater than the sum of our parts. We are [name of group].

(The leader now recites the name of each person, alternating with the name of the group, like *Deborah. Mooncircle. Joe. Mooncircle. Tate. Mooncircle,* encouraging everyone to join in. After one or two rounds, you can dance, drum, or whatever, allowing all the names—group and individual—to merge into a chant. If people screw up the word order, it doesn't matter. It just reinforces the blending of self with other. Allow this to go on as long as feels right.)

Leader: *We are individuals. We are [group name]. We are apart. We are joined. We are blessed. So be it.*

All: *So be it!*

Journal/Discussion Prompts

- Did you notice yourself as an isolated Self at the beginning of the ritual? Did that feel different at the end?
- Did you notice a relationship to others in the circle as Other at the beginning of the ritual? Did that feel different at the end?
- What did the experience of being in a group feel like? How did that change the experience of Self? Of Other?

Chapter Nine

Passive and Active

The polarity of passive/active contains a strong connection to that of force/form, as mentioned in chapter 7. Here it is more earth-based and more practical. While force and form are cosmic principles of creation, passive and active are manifest in behavior; they are both spiritual and ordinary.

As with the other polarities we've discussed, there's a socially gendered component to passive/active. In the patriarchy, women are expected to be passive, to be acted upon rather than act independently. I'd add that this is true for any marginalized group. Whether we're talking about people of color, immigrants, disabled people, or queer people, the majority expects the minority to wait around politely to be given civil rights or even basic humanity. Stereotypes like "angry Black woman" arise from the notion that the active role is the inherent right only of the powerful.

Energetically, passive/active takes us right back to our science lesson: electrons rush toward protons, while protons hold still and wait. The passive pole here is creating a space where it is safe for the active party to arrive. If they were rushing toward each other at equal speed, that would be quite the crash on meeting! Instead, we can see the passive energy as kind of feathering the nest, opening a receptive safety net in which the active energy can land. The passive pole has to have great strength in order to absorb the active pole when it arrives; in fact, they must have equal strength. If passive is stronger, it swallows up the active; and if active is stronger, it breaks the passive.

In my younger, gender-essentialist days, I saw beauty in the passive role. Now that I am better educated and reject gender essentialism, I still see that beauty, I just don't attach gender to it. There is genuinely grace in letting go of will, and receiving the will of another, in reaching within to find strength in patience and in trust.

The passive pole, by itself, accomplishes nothing—virtually by definition. It *is* and does not *do*. Passive energy is a deep pool from which active energy can draw. The active pole, by itself, runs dry; it lacks a source. Active is fueled by energy, movement, excitement, arousal, and so on, but it requires stillness and calm to renew itself and maintain that energy and movement. Passive without active is helpless; active without passive is empty.

The Third

The third of passive/active is a creation. When we look at the other polarities in the next section, we'll see that some passive/active polarity metaphors are heteronormative and can be perceived as procreation or agriculture. But the third of passive/active can also be an admixture, as in the (active) ingredients that are mixed in a (passive) bowl. In this way, it is certainly a whole greater than the sum of its parts: a loaf of bread is neither flour nor bowl nor rolling pin. The energy created by passive/active polarity spills out into the world in unexpected ways. Part of the beauty of forming this kind of energy is that you don't necessarily know what will manifest.

Contrarily, the active party can choose the goal/creation and the passive party can consent to it, and then the polar energy can be worked to manifest that goal: thesis, antithesis, synthesis.

Other Polarities That Are Passive/Active

I moved **stasis and movement** back and forth between this section and force/form a few times. After all, geography holds still (except over millennia), while history inexorably moves. Stasis and movement are at the root of polarity, a part of its core nature. Electrons move and protons hold still—we're at the beginning of understanding poles when we talk about this pair. In that sense, you can probably find traces of stasis/movement energy in *every* polarity. This pairing shows us the extraordinary strength necessary in passivity: the irresistible force cannot be said to be more powerful than the immovable object.

And again, stasis is absolutely necessary for movement to be meaningful. The patriarchy tends to make qualities associated with men seem more powerful, more interesting, and definitely cooler. This is certainly true with movement, which is what a Man of Action does while the Damsel in Distress holds still and waits for him. So it's important to see that the imbalance of these ideas isn't just a problem because of sexism; it's a problem because of the imbalance itself.

It's possible that no polarity is more deeply tied to gender essentialism than that of **fucked**[134] **and fucker.** It's hard even to come up with polite terminology for it. We can say *intercourse* or *lovemaking*, but that doesn't explore the subject/object relationship of penetration. *Only* vulgar language is common for that, which I think is because the concept is deeply connected to things like misogyny and our fears about how a misogynist culture treats not just women, but anyone perceived as womanly.

To be penetrated is to be feminine, and when a man is penetrated, he is seen as feminized. To penetrate is seen as masculine, and a woman who penetrates is seen as manly. For the homophobe, feminized men are terrifying and masculinized women are repulsive.

If you think about it, homophobic language, jokes, slurs, and slang all revolve around men being fucked. There's no visceral terror of oral sex, for example. The horror is that a man will be on the receiving end of treatment reserved for women. Sex columnist Dan Savage has said:

> I think a lot of homophobia is hatred of women repackaged, 'cause gay men seem to preoccupy homophobes the most. It's usually

---

134. My mother said *fuckee* the other day, but I'm sticking with *fucked*.

about anal sex, and gay men are perceived as taking on the woman's role, and women are despised. The woman's role is less-than. And in a male-supremacy culture, men who take on the woman's role willingly kind of freak out some of the dudes.[135]

This goes as far as the idea that men who penetrate other men are seen as "not really gay"—they're just doing what they need to do, and the man being fucked is as disconnected from real desire as the pie in *American Pie*.

Savage regularly gets letters from readers along the lines of "I'm a man. I'm not attracted to men in any way and I've never slept with a man. I love when my wife penetrates me with a dildo. Am I gay?" On the face of it, the question is ludicrous. How can a man who isn't into other men be gay? But *being penetrated* is the key here. Homophobia tells us that gay men are abnormal because they're womanly at some level. Gender essentialism tells us that a man who wants to be fucked is womanly. Q.E.D.

Why does any of this matter to us? Because the gender essentialism and the misogyny and—implicitly—the potential violence of fucker/fucked as a polarity completely distort our ability to understand its powerful magic.

The fucker/fucked polarity aligns with others such as **socket/plug** and **receptive/projective.** The power of receiving here is maligned when it is "fucked," but it is obviously essential. Plugs don't work without sockets, but once they are two they are a greater whole. Projective magic only works when there is a receiving end. Projective *anything* only works when there is a receiving end. As long as we carry an unconscious bias against fucked/receptive/passive, we fail to understand a depth of magic that demands us to wait, trust, receive, and hold still.

The most transcendent polarity associated with passive/active is that of **being and becoming.** This is so woo-woo that it might belong with force and form, but I like it here because of the way it empowers the passive pole and also because *form* and *being* aren't tightly cognate. Force can also simply "be." Becoming is movement and growth; none of us wants to look at our lives as holding still. On the other hand, "just be" is a meditative

---

135. Robinson, "Dan Savage."

guide; none of us thrives when we must constantly go-go-go and become the next thing.

Deities of Passivity and Activity

In Welsh myth, the love goddess **Branwen** was given in marriage to Matholwch. He began to mistreat her and imprisoned travelers so that they could not return to her brother, **Bran the Blessed**, with news of her condition. Branwen trained a bird (variously said to be a crow or starling) to send a message to her brother, and then had to passively wait for rescue. The imprisoned goddess, who must simply wait yet has the power to raise an army, has powerful polarity energy. A similar example is found in **Helen** and **Paris.** Helen of Troy was originally a vegetation goddess, but in the story of the *Iliad*, she is a passive principle, acted upon by Paris, who nonetheless gathers the massive activity of the Trojan War around her.[136]

In a completely different vein, I'm fond of **Pasiphae** and the **Sacred Bull** as an example of the perversity of the fucker/fucked polarity. In this Cretan myth, Pasiphae desired the bull and mated with him. Legend has it that she had **Daedalus** create a cow-body for her to allow this to occur. She is *active* in choosing the "fucked" role, which really queers the mythology. It's interesting that this is the second time we see Daedalus, and his inventions, as a mediating space in a polarity, here between Pasiphae and the bull, and in self/other between Helios and Icarus.

Kabbalistically, passive and active can be seen as corresponding to **Keter** and **Malkut.** Keter is the original activation of the Tree of Life; as the first sephirah, it is the source of all activity. Malkut is the receptacle of all Kabbalistic energy, which emanates from Keter, travels through the Tree, and arrives at Malkut; thus Malkut passively receives.

Passive and Active in Humanity

The problem with the passive/active polarity in humans is that it manifests in strict social rules about who has permission to be active. When only

---

136. Monaghan, *The Book of Goddesses & Heroines*, 151–52.

men are active in the world and women are required to be passive, both activity and passivity become distorted and hurtful.

"Passive-aggressive" behavior is resistance or protest that is nonconfrontational. It is often the only resort for someone in a situation of required passivity, although certainly it's not *only* a by-product of social mores. To be passive-aggressive is to fail to act when that failure hurts or upsets someone else. Promising to do something important and then not doing it, or doing it poorly, are classic examples. It's characterized both by its hostility and its deniability: "I just forgot." Someone might be passive-aggressive for any number of reasons, but one such reason is that it's their only available means of saying no. When active refusal is denied, passive-aggressive behavior is what's left.

If someone passively refuses to do something as a voiced protest, you wouldn't call that passive-aggressive because it's voiced. In a society in which women are expected to passively provide services to men, a fight might manifest as withholding those services (such as cooking, laundry, or sex). Even withholding conversation (the silent treatment) can be a protest by a person required to be passive against a person required to be active.

I've talked mostly about the passive pole because passivity is marginalized: it is both designated as the behavior of marginalized people and is treated as an unworthy sort of behavior. Heroes *act*. But being forced into the active role, with no outlet, is also harmful, provoking anxiety, frustration, or violence.

None of this has anything to do with the potential energy created by a shared and consensual experience of passive/active polarity. Indeed, having some passive/active polarity in a relationship is normal. A pair of active people is like a comedy routine about two people holding the door for each other or, contrarily, both going through the door at the same time; both involve bumping and awkwardness and not a whole lot of actually getting through the door. A pair of passive people is like the old "lesbian sheep" joke: Did you know that the way that ewes flirt is by holding very still so that the rams know they're interested? Then what do lesbian sheep do? Not much.

Passive/active polarity in a relationship is empowering when it is agreeable to both parties, and when both are able to express their natural need for both passivity and activity.

Consider certain disabilities in which a person might need to passively wait to be helped. Living an active, empowered life requires dependency on a home health aide for some people, for example, a wheelchair user who needs to be assisted into their chair. They're active once in the chair, but until then, there's an enforced passivity that can be frustrating, even infuriating. This seems like a paradox: I am independent by being dependent, active by being passive. Rather than a paradox, though, it's a *polarity*; it's a movement of energy enabled by a recognition that the poles are connected. I'm not telling any disabled person to be happy about a difficult situation, but it can be powerful to find that energy is there for the taking.

The passive/active pole is perhaps the only important polarity that most people are intuitively able to connect to within themselves without need for a partner. As individuals, we know that too much "active" is draining and that just *being*, rather than doing/becoming all the time, is renewing. Vacation time is time for just being.

As noted in chapter 2, creating a solitary polarity has long been seen as highly advanced work. Yet in day-to-day life many of us are pretty good at switching poles from active to passive. We do this by being active in one arena and then shifting focus onto another. If your work is mental or verbal, physical activity can help you switch the poles internally; you're turning the mentally active switch to *off* by focusing active energy on the physical, which is one reason exercise can be such a relief from stress. On the rare occasions that I have writer's block, I do something creatively nonverbal, such as beading—something that involves color and touch. It allows me to place words in a passive state, letting the well fill back up slowly. It's choosing a passive stance in my language centers by moving my active state entirely away from language. This allows my language skills to renew the well of passivity and draw from it.

Simply going on vacation is one means of enacting the shift from passive to active. Recently my day job became particularly overwhelming, and

I started to feel real burnout. The active pole was emptying out, unable to be renewed by the passive pole: classic overwork. On vacation, lazing by the pool, not even doing "fun" activities beyond enjoying the sun and water, I found renewal. I was tempted to write about the experience as polar *while* I was on vacation, but realized it was counterproductive—the urge to action can rob passivity of its power!

Magical Tools of Passive and Active

Tools of passive and active can be the same as tools of force and form. Just as the sword projects force, it is also seen as active. Just as the cup creates form, it is also seen as passive. Since sword/knife and cup are quintessentially force/form in Wicca, I'd use the wand and pentacle as passive/active in that tradition.

Any tool used for an *activity* can be seen as active, such as a sickle or boleen or aspergillum. Any tool used to be *receptive*, such as a scrying bowl or mirror or a crystal ball, can be seen as passive.

In Tibetan Buddhism, the bell and the dorje (a ritual weapon) are ritual objects representing female/space/wisdom and male/power/reality, respectively. I like how these highly symbolic and complicated ritual tools each have passive and active components. The bell exists in time—it creates a sound that has a beginning and an end—whereas the dorje is eternal. Contrarily, the bell is passively listened to, while the dorje is actively moved (spun in the hand in some rituals).

In Crowley's *777*, the tool of Keter is the crown (Keter means "crown" in Hebrew) and Malkut is the magic circle or triangle.[137] It is interesting to imagine a ritual of coronation taking place in a magic circle, or perhaps crowning a deity or deity representative, as a passive/active polarity ritual, with Passive giving the crown to Active and then ceding the active power to them.

---

137. Crowley, *777*, page 13 of *Book Two*.

Passive and Active in Ritual

In any partnership, there is an ongoing component of passive/active at play. The role taken is generally not constant and switches back and forth often, even moment by moment. Nonetheless, the polar energy is there: One person acts, and one person holds space and waits for that person to act. Perhaps one surprises the other, and the passive partner is the recipient of that surprise. This is true in normal human relationships and also in ritual relationships. I invoke upon you, I hand you a magical wand, I recite a trance induction, I anoint you with oil. In each of these acts, I am active and you are passive. In some, we might immediately switch. I might hand you the oil to anoint me in turn, for example. The passive/active energy is exchanged quickly, almost invisibly, but it is exchanged.

In an invocation of a deity into the body of a recipient, the person doing the invocation is not entirely the "active partner," so much as an agent of the active deity. Nonetheless, it is my experience that such rituals work best when the person invoking is treated as the active partner. During the Wiccan ritual of drawing down the moon, in which the Goddess is invoked by the high priest into the body of the high priestess, I find it most effective when the coven sends energy not primarily into the priestess but into the priest. Invocation is the act of magic being performed, and energy is being sent into the magic. The priestess is the *recipient* or *target* of the magic, not the magician. (These genders are traditional in the rite described but aren't meant to be prescriptive here. A ritual that isn't gender normative might call both partners *priestex*, or it might retain the priest/priestess designation but not the deity-to-human gender correspondences.)

In a passive/active energy exchange, the active partner makes a lot of choices: forceful or gentle, teasingly withholding or direct, controlling or accommodating. Because the passive partner is holding space in a state of consent and trust, the active partner is empowered to experiment with different ways of using and manipulating the active energy.

The Passive/Active Ritual

The intention of this ritual is to intensify the experience and energy of the passive/active polarity by concentrating and accentuating it. Recalling chapter 2 where we discussed how polarity can be deepened by contrast or sublimation, we'll focus on contrast here, forcing a constant exchange between passive and active and back again.

In the force/form ritual in chapter 7, Force was functionally passive, in that it was Form who actually cast the circle, sprinkled it with salt water, etc. The phrase "Force silently sends power" was repeated. Nonetheless, the force partner was *actively* creating and sending energy, while the form partner was *actively* performing ritual steps. The intention here is to lean into the passivity, to experience not sending force but rather opening space and being patient, creating an energy vortex into which the active energy floods, filling the space to overflowing, which then allows the passive partner to act using that energy. Once that action is taken, the next moment of passivity occurs, and the cycle repeats.

As with the force/form ritual, the energy of the passive/active polarity can be added to any ritual you already do.

Because passively waiting for the next step can be awkward or frustrating, it is essential to begin by connecting with your partner.

Preparing for the Passive/Active before Ritual

Passive and Active: Breathe deeply while making eye contact with each other. Hold hands or not as you feel comfortable. Find a connected rhythm where your gaze and your breath become one. Know that you trust this person, and that you share this polar energy freely with them.

Active: Focus on respect for your partner and honor for their trust in you. Give yourself permission to enjoy this power in ways that are playful or dramatic, direct or teasing.

Passive: Focus on openness and trust. Breathe into your own patience and stillness. Find yourself giving your partner permission to be exactly who they are and how they are.

Active: (Now blindfolds the passive partner.)

Note that the use of the blindfold is optional. The purpose is to emphasize, for both partners, Passive's need to wait for and trust the active partner. If the blindfold provokes anxiety or terror, it is not helpful and shouldn't be used.

Example: Consecrating the Four Elements

Passive: *It is time to consecrate the elements.* (This is the signal to Active that all power is being given over to them to direct the energy for this task. Passive waits, opening a space for receiving Active's next action.)

Active: *We will consecrate Air.* (Note that here Active can control the order of consecrations as well as the pacing, although the tradition you work may have a specified order.)

Active: (Lifts incense or other Air symbol and presents it to Passive, visualizing active energy flowing into the space Passive has created, flowing into it and overflowing out of it, into the Air as it is consecrated. If Passive is blindfolded, Active will guide Passive's hand to show them where the incense is, or place it in their hand.)

Passive: *Air, element of wisdom and inspiration, be consecrated by the power we raise here.* (Passive feels the overflow of energy into the incense as they consecrate. As Passive waits for Active to take away the Air and present the next element, they again focus on trust and space for Active.)

Active: *We will consecrate Fire.* (Lifts candle or other Fire symbol and presents it to Passive, again visualizing energy as before. If Passive is blindfolded, Active will guide Passive's hand to show them where the candle is, or place it in their hand.)

Passive: *Fire, element of will and passion, be consecrated by the power we raise here.* (Repeat the visualization of overflowing energy followed by trust and space.)

Active: *We will consecrate Water.* (Lifts water dish or other Water symbol and presents it to Passive with the same visualization and guidance.)

Passive: *Water, element of emotion and mystery, be consecrated by the power we raise here.* (Repeat the visualization.)

Active: *We will consecrate Earth.* (Lifts salt dish or other Earth symbol and presents it to Passive with the same visualization and guidance.)

Passive: *Earth, element of the body and foundation, be consecrated by the power we raise here.* (Repeat the visualization.)

Journal/Discussion Prompts

- How did it feel to hold space as the passive partner? Did you find it stressful? Was trusting your partner easy or difficult? What did you find in that space?
- How did it feel to have the power of the active partner? Did you trust yourself? Did you have feelings or thoughts about your passive partner? About the energy?
- Knowing that many magical traditions attribute gender to active and passive, did you experience any such gender connection during the ritual?
- Did you have a preference for the active or passive role?
- In rituals that you already do, where does an active/passive polarity already exist?

A Solitary Ritual of Active/Passive

As mentioned earlier in this chapter in the section "Passive and Active in Humanity," this is one pole in which people tend to be good at building an inner circuit, but we're not often conscious of it. By creating a simple solitary ritual for moving energy between the poles of passive and active, we can empower this energy shift and this circuit.

YOU'LL NEED

- Your altar (on which to place everything)
- A tool of each pole (perhaps a wand for the active pole and a pentacle for the passive pole)
- A symbol of the active function you're allowing to rest (In my personal example, I could use a pen to symbolize writing.)
- A symbol of the alternate active function you're moving to in order to complete the circuit (For me, that might be a set of colored pencils for drawing or some beads.)

STEPS

1. Pick up the symbol of the active function that needs a rest (the pen, for example). While holding it, visualize the intense active energy that has poured forth from it.

2. Look at the tool of the passive pole (such as the pentacle). Visualize its stillness. Feel its quiet and its passivity. Holding your active symbol (the pen), place it on the passive tool. Visualize its energy moving and flowing into the tool. Visualize the energy coming to rest there.

3. Say: Beloved [name of the active symbol, such as pen], it is time to rest. Beloved [symbol], it is time to renew. Be at peace. Your work can cease. Renew, renew, and return when renewed.

4. Now pick up the symbol of the alternate function (the beads). Visualize it as having been still, in stasis, at rest. It is fully rested and ready to act. It is brimming with the dark, pooling energy of the passive pole.

5. Place this symbol of the passive pole back on the altar.

6. Pick up the tool of the active pole (such as the wand). Visualize it vibrating with energy and the will to act. Visualize its joy of pushing forward. Point the tool at the symbol of the passive pole (beads, etc.) and see its energy rushing forth into the symbol, enlivening it.

7. Say: *Beloved [name of the symbol of the alternate function, such as beads], awaken. Beloved [symbol], be active. Let's do, let's act. It is time to awaken; your work can begin. Awaken, awaken, and rest when complete.*

8. Place the wand (tool of the active pole) back on the altar so that it is touching the pentacle (tool of the passive pole).

9. Visualize the flow of movement, active to passive and back again, as moving between the tools and between the symbols.

10. When you're ready, say: *It is done. So be it.*

Journal/Discussion Prompts

• What is it you do that can be too active in your life? Does this activity benefit when you give it a rest?

• Are you able to visualize renewal of the activity through allowing it to be passive?

• What alternate activities exist in your life that are renewing for you?

• Did the ritual allow you to experience the flow of active to passive?

• What do you need to do in your own life to renew yourself? Does it lend itself to this ritual?

Chapter Ten

Dominance and Submission

It's not my intention for this chapter to be exclusively about dominance and submission as a sexual kink, or for it to be accessible only to people who have that kink. Nonetheless, I should probably define the kink, for those unfamiliar, up front. We'll be talking about it more in this chapter, and certainly people who *are* into BDSM will appreciate combining their existing experience with polarity work.

BDSM is both an abbreviation and a portmanteau of three other abbreviations. It combines *B&D*: bondage and discipline; *D&S* or *D/s*: dominance and submission; and *S&M*: sadism and masochism. Each can be considered its own kink, but since there's a lot of overlap, BDSM was coined. *Bondage and discipline* refers specifically to the physical act of bondage as well as any accompanying psychological or verbal discipline, while *dominance and submission* refers to any psychological, verbal, or physical dominance/submission scenarios. Either B&D or D&S can involve pain. S&M is often used to designate the purely physical: pain-for-pleasure scenarios that may not have a psychological or playacting component. Since all these bleed into each other, BDSM is a sensible term.

Energetically, *dominance* and *submission* are a polarity in part because one does not exist without the other: you have to have someone to dominate; someone to whom to submit. These aren't activities or states of being that make sense in isolation. Domination must flow to the submissive and vice versa.

Of the top-level polarities in this book (meaning the chapter headings/ groupings under which I've organized all the polarities discussed), *only* dominance and submission inherently require the presence of the other pole.

We've already discussed (in chapter 1) the way in which polarity is relative; the existence of a polarity inherently requires both poles. Gray is dark compared to white but is light compared to black. "Dark" doesn't exist by itself, but only in relation to a contrasting pole. But the qualities that exist on the poles we've explored can and do exist in isolation.

It's perfectly feasible for force to exist without form, or for form to exist without force. One is chaotic and one is inert; only together do they create. Yet they can *be*. Similarly, passivity can exist without activity, and activity can be ceaseless, without a passive break. One is nonproductive and one leads to burnout, but they are possible. Continuing on, night can exist without day. If a planet's orbit on its axis took the same length of time as its orbit of its sun—meaning that a day and a year were the same length—then one side of the planet would always face the sun and one side never would. There would be a hemisphere of endless day and one of endless night. Finally, genders can exist in isolation—only a heteronormative binary leads us to believe that *female* implies the existence of *male*.

Self and other is a polarity of perception. As a self, I *perceive* other. Other exists only as a concept held by self and cannot exist on its own. But self can certainly exist without perceiving other—that's narcissism in a nutshell.

Only in the polarity of dominance and submission are both poles meaningless without the presence of the other. They are a locked pair. Just as *dark* and *light* are relative, so are *above* and *below*, so that the use of *top* and *bottom* as analogous terms for *dominant* and *submissive* is significant.

The power flow in dominance and submission is incredibly dynamic. In BDSM, *power exchange* refers to the submissive giving power and the dominant receiving it. It sounds straightforward, but anyone who's done it in real life will tell you it's anything but. The submissive, in many ways, is calling the shots; setting the boundaries about how far they're willing to go, what their boundaries are, and what is off-limits. The submissive gives power to the dominant only after first asserting this power of setting boundaries and limits.

From that point, yes, absolutely, the submissive gives power in a profound way. Depending on the relationship, a submissive might cede authority to their dominant regarding what they wear, eat, and say, and might be required to consent to any and all sexual demands or physical punishment—provided, of course, it is within the boundaries the submissive has previously set. Service might also include things like housework. So from the submissive side, power is held, explored, and then freely given. Naturally, the submissive can also end the agreement at any time.

Dominance in such a relationship is also complicated. First, of course, the dominant must cede power before receiving it, just as the submissive has it before giving it. More significantly, a submissive, having given up power, is in a helpless position, and it is the dominant's responsibility to care for them. A simple example: In a bondage scene, the dominant has to make sure the submissive is safe, their circulation isn't impaired, and their nerves aren't being pinched. Moreover, the experience of powerlessly undergoing both pain and pleasure often puts the submissive in an altered state of consciousness (kinksters call it *subspace*). Having been through an ordeal, possibly a mind-altering one, submissives require "aftercare." Thus, the dominant is in a position of serving the submissive's needs, which seems on the surface to be a reversal of the expected power positions and energy flow. Any dominant will tell you that dominance is a lot of work, and a good dominant does, in fact, serve the submissive. As *Sacred Kink* puts it:

Mastery is also a path of spiritual submission.[138] I am called to stretch the boundaries of my greatness and potential not through

---

138. The distinction between a master/slave relationship, a dominant/submissive relationship, a top/bottom relationship, and other terminology is very "inside baseball" if you're not a part of the BDSM world. I refer the reader to Lee Harrington's *Sacred Kink* for a detailed discussion of this and many other subjects, as well as a robust bibliography.

ego, but through surrender. Mastery is a form of service, to the universe, to ourselves, to those we are in charge of. Giving and receiving service is a dance. The service that I give may have no resemblance on the surface to the service my Slave gives me, but they are both serving a greater good.[139]

This dance, to me, is the heart of polarity: Dominance is service, service is strength, and the dance of energies creates a power given to the universe—as an offering, for magic, or for some other purpose.

The Third

When thinking about the polarity of dominance and submission, the first "third" that comes to mind is harmony. In its simplest form, when one party dominates willingly and the other submits willingly, they together eliminate disagreement. If a deciding vote is needed, they both always know whose vote that is. The dominant votes, the submissive accedes, and an accord is reached.

The liminal space between dominance and submission is equity. In perfect equality, no one dominates and no one submits. As power is exchanged back and forth between these poles, equity is continually traversed. Its energy is there to partake of.

Wholeness is also a product of dominance and submission. I struggle with this, because "wholeness" sounds facile—like it could apply to any polarity. Perhaps it therefore sounds meaningless. But dominance and submission are, in their best sense, a form of cooperation for a greater purpose, in which harmony is achieved so that the purpose can be served. Of course, because these are the poles that cannot exist without the other, they are also the poles that cannot be whole without the other.

The third can also be an offering. Religious people—monotheists as well as Pagans and polytheists—often allow God/the gods to dominate them. Yoga is a "yoke," a discipline of bondage, of service to God, *restraining* the mind. Even in a power exchange with a deity, though, there is still

---

139. Harrington, *Sacred Kink*, 311.

a back-and-forth. A relationship with a deity does not mean being enslaved to that deity; it's okay, and often necessary, to experience a deity telling you something and respond, "No, thank you."

The energy runs from the dominant (person, spirit, or deity), who facilitates the raising of energy from the submissive, generating the third, which is an offering of some sort. The submissive feeds energy back to the dominant, often simply in the form of willing service, perhaps in love and gratitude, certainly in submission itself.

Another way of seeing this dominant/submissive relationship with deity is in a trance ritual where a person receives the presence of a deity into their body (such as drawing down the moon in Wicca or being "ridden" in Voudon). The human is *submitting* to the use of their body by the deity, and the deity is dominant. The third, then, is the blessings or message shared by the deity with the worshipers.

If you think of BDSM, the third can be the "scene" itself. The submissive might have a goal—as mundane as sexual release, but perhaps a transformative and mind-altering experience, or perhaps healing in the form of undergoing an ordeal. The release/experience/healing is a third facilitated by the dominant, elicited via the scene from the submissive. The energy of the BDSM experience is given over to this third.

In BDSM, it's important that the circuit be completed, and the submissive give energy back to the dominant. It's easy for a dominant to become burnt out, since they give so much to the submissive, if energy is not returned. Thus, rituals of the submissive worshiping, adoring, and serving the dominant complete an energetic loop.

Or the submissive might be a solitary worshiper at the altar of a dominant deity, giving an offering of submission to create a third of harmony with the deity.

Other Polarities That Are Dominance/Submission

As mentioned above, **top** and **bottom** are often used as shorthand for a BDSM relationship (or can be descriptive of a relationship that is primarily physical, without a psychological aspect). Top and bottom are also used to describe sexual relationships, which will be covered in chapter 13.

Control and **surrender** is a polarity closely tied to dominance and submission. Dominance is control over a situation or person (including the self). Surrender is releasing the need for control—again, including over the self. Ecstasy and abandon are states of surrender, while focus and concentration are states of control. These are often called **Apollonian** and **Dionysian**. Meditation, ritual, gatherings, and even theology tend to exist somewhere along a continuum of Apollonian to Dionysian. Seeing it as a polarity, with energy being exchanged along that continuum, can be empowering and can certainly help us appreciate and understand people "doing" their p-word practices in ways we just don't relate to. A similar polarity is **order** and **chaos**; clearly we can see that neither is fully creative without the other. Chaos, like force, is just the energy, while order is just the form.

Often, we have good ideas that we want to implement—a business to start, a book to write, a home to decorate, a child to raise. But we have to allow for and permit chaos in order for manifestation to happen—the market conditions change, creative energy takes the book in a different direction, available fabric colors inspire change, a child has a will of their own. Rigidity destroys the creative process, even as chaos without some form of order prevents creativity from manifesting in the real world.

Here is also where **center** and **circumference** make their appearance, as promised in chapter 8. The dominant, controlling energy forms a stable center, and this stability tethers the submissive, who thus has permission to be completely ungrounded. Because the submissive doesn't have to ground themselves, because a polar partner is holding that space, ecstatic abandon—reaching the ends of the available space (the circumference)—is possible.

In astral travel, the traveler is taught to clearly visualize a silver cord connecting the spirit to the body, and to practice following the cord back home. You can travel as far as you like as long as you have that cord to lead you back to your body. Without the cord, you can get lost, like Hansel and

Gretel, unable to follow the trail back home. In the polarity of center and circumference, one partner serves the function of the silver cord, holding the center and guiding the other partner back. Only because they know they can return, only because of the center, can the circumference explore their own limits.

Suppose the circumference/chaos that a submissive wishes to explore is screaming. They long to be able to just let their voice go completely and scream their head off. The dominant facilitates that by gagging them, so that the screaming occurs behind the gag (where it won't alarm the neighbors), or by soundproofing a space for them to play, or by taking them to a remote location with no neighbors or some other safe space. The dominant provides a center/structure in which the chaos can occur.

Deities of Dominance and Submission

It is a curious fact that one of the primary mythological forms in which the polarity of dominance and submission is visible is that of encounters with Death. It seems that death (or "Age and Fate," as we'll see in a moment) is the primary thing that a deity must humbly submit themselves to.

Persephone is kidnapped (humbled, dominated) by **Hades** in a tale mediated by **Demeter**. Because of Demeter's intervention, Persephone remains both the maiden **Koré** and the goddess of the underworld. In a separate tale, Hades also forces **Orpheus** to submit to his will and the inevitability of death.

Inanna, goddess of Sumer, descends to confront her sister **Erishkegal**, goddess of death. Inanna enters, "As tall as heaven/As wide as the earth,"[140] and wearing royal raiments. But Erishkegal gives instructions that Inanna's raiments be stripped from her: "Let the holy priestess of heaven enter bowed low."[141] Inanna is rescued by creatures "neither male nor female,"[142] who can be seen as mediating forces.

---

140. Wolkstein and Kramer, *Inanna, Queen of Heaven and Earth*, 56.

141. Wolkstein and Kramer, *Inanna, Queen of Heaven and Earth*, 57.

142. Wolkstein and Kramer, *Inanna, Queen of Heaven and Earth*, 64.

When rescued, Inanna must find a replacement for herself in the land of death, and chooses her husband, **Dumuzi**, who didn't mourn her. In a separate story, we learn that Dumuzi's sister, **Geshtinanna**,[143] sacrificed half her life for him so that each could live in the underworld for half the year. As with Persephone and Demeter, the need to humble oneself before death is mediated by a family member, with agricultural implications. Dominance and submission, in mythology, are tied to death and rebirth.

Another version of the descent to the underworld is found originating in Wicca, published in numerous sources, beginning with Gerald Gardner. Here "**the Witch Goddess**" descends to confront "**Death the Mighty One**." She is humbled, like Inanna, and bound. Death says he is helpless to "Age and Fate" and cannot save her creatures. Since she refuses to accept him, she is made to kneel and is scourged, "and she cried 'I feel the pangs of love.'"[144]

When we look at polarities of chaos and order, we can see the deities for whom they are sometimes named: **Apollo** and **Dionysus**. Interestingly, Dionysus has a connection to the Persephone/Hades myth: he is seen as a polar counterpart to Hades, just as Demeter and Persephone are known throughout classical mythology as "the two who are one." Demeter refuses to drink wine because of Dionysus's connection to both wine and Hades; the mysteries of Demeter involve a barley-based drink instead.

Another place that dominance and submission shows up in mythology is in acts of penance. **Hera** drives **Herakles** (Hercules) mad,[145] causing him to murder his wife, Megara, and their children. He prays to **Apollo** and is given the penance of service to King Eurystheus, who imposes upon him the "12 labors." Here, Hera is the agent of chaos (madness) and Apollo restores order. But additionally, Hera dominates Herakles, who must submit to enslavement for a time in order to restore himself to wholeness.

My friend Jack Chanek pointed out to me that **Pwyll** and **Rhiannon** are a dominant/submissive pair in Welsh mythology. Pwyll sees Rhiannon

143. Monaghan, *The Book of Goddesses & Heroines*, 133.

144. Gardner, *The Meaning of Witchcraft*, 265.

145. Madeleine. "What Were the 12 Labors of Hercules?"

riding her horse and tries to chase her but cannot catch her. When he asks her to please stop, she gladly does so. She demands that Pwyll *not* dominate her, and says she is escaping an arranged marriage for a love match with Pwyll.[146] She asserts her freedom and refuses domination. Later, she is falsely accused of devouring her own child (although Rhiannon, as an underworld goddess, may well have actually committed infanticide in a more primitive version of the myth[147]). As penance, Rhiannon must tell her tale to all who come to the gates of the city and carry them inside on her back. Symbolically, she went from riding a horse that cannot be caught to being one perpetually caught herself, as well as going from being indomitable to the lowliest of servants. Again, this penance exists to eventually restore her to her rightful queenship.

These are just two examples of many legends of gods and rulers submitting to penance—shifting from dominance to submission—in order to restore wholeness or order.

In the Kabbalah, dominance corresponds to **Gevurah** (strength) and submission corresponds to **Chesed** (lovingkindness). Although the word *gevurah* has a female ending and is on the female-aligned Pillar of Severity, Gevurah and Chesed are often thought of as the two manifestations of "father"—the stern judge and the indulgent papa: the one who punishes, frightens, disciplines, and limits and the one who forgives, embraces, and allows.

Dominance and Submission in Humanity

In human relations, dominance and submission do not just exist as a fetish. If they didn't exist in ordinary life, there would be no power in ritualizing, formalizing, or sexualizing them as a fetish.

Parents dominate children out of necessity. A parent who doesn't dominate their children is basically abrogating the responsibilities of parenthood. Yes, children need a voice in their own lives, but part of a parent's dominance is in determining how much and where that is allowed. Yet

---

146. Rolleston, *Celtic Myths and Legends*, 360–64.

147. Monaghan, *The Book of Goddesses & Heroines*, 297.

anyone who has dealt with children knows that being a parent is also being utterly run by the little monarchs of their domain. To have a child is to be dominated by the person you dominate.

Everywhere in human relations, dominance manifests as service. To manage (dominate) a restaurant is to be in service to your customers, and to be a customer is both to submit (to the menu, to the quality of service, to the chef) and to dominate (everything you request is a demand, and everything you demand is a request). The complexity of dominance and submission in a simple restaurant encounter is reflected in a myriad of human interactions that purport to be straightforward.

Dominance and submission also exist in a hierarchy. In a corporate structure, for example, few of us are at the very top or the very bottom, so there's someone taking our orders, someone giving orders to us, and someone lateral to us with whom we interact, without dominance or submission, though we are impacted by them just the same. At the top of the corporate food chain, the CEO is beholden to the board of directors, the shareholders (if any), and the unions (if any), so a bit of a circle is sketched. While the politics of late-stage capitalism increasingly skews those relationships, the underlying energy remains.

In religion, dominance and submission are not just between the dominant deity (or deities) and the submissive worshiper. Most religions have institutional hierarchies. Indeed, many people have come to p-word paths thoroughly sick of the authoritarian nature of the religions of their youth. Yet the subtle flow of energy along this polarity is as true in religious groups as anywhere else.

I am a Wiccan priestess. While it is certainly true that some people—probably far too many—abuse such a position, it is also true that it is a position of service. Yes, I am often the dominant force in my coven, although it's hard to tell if that's because of my (socially dominant, extroverted, kind of loud) personality rather than my role. But I am also given over to service, submitting to the needs of my coveners and candidates. At the same time, candidates are submitting to a group or group leaders who have something they want—the coven itself—and perhaps it seems to them that they're jumping through hoops to get in. While I am in service to these seekers, they might certainly see themselves as utterly dominated by me, and indeed, they're not wrong. There are rules in my group that you submit to, and you can be booted out for misbehavior. These are very reasonable rules (no abusive behavior, no violating confidentiality, showing up when you say you will), but they're rules nonetheless.

Even the most egalitarian and consensus-driven p-word groups have some form of boundary enforcement, some dividing line between "in" and "out," which means that those on the outside wishing to get in must be submissive to the dominance of that boundary.

An initiation or dedication ceremony often ritualizes that submission, with the candidate submitting to the guidance or dominance of those already inside. From coming-of-age ceremonies to shamanic ordeals to entry into the Masons, the candidate submits, and those who have already gone through the ritual dominate. Meanwhile, the energy flow is from the initiator into the candidate; energy is being used to transform the candidate into an initiate (the child into an adult, the outsider into an insider, etc.).

Magical Tools of Dominance and Submission

Crowley's 777 gives the tools of Chesed as wand, sceptre, or crook, while Gevurah gets the sword, spear, scourge, or chain.[148] The crook and flail (scourge) are the symbols of the god Osiris. The crook is the symbol of the shepherd and represents guidance, while the flail can represent punishment (whipping). Another interpretation is that the crook is husbandry (it's the tool of a shepherd) and the flail is agriculture (it's used to thresh wheat). Together, they represent kingship.

The scourge and cords appear as tools in the Wiccan legend of the descent of the Witch Goddess to the underworld; the scourge is the dominant tool, wielded by Death the Mighty One. The cords are the submissive tool, as the Goddess kneels and is bound in submission.

---

148. Crowley, 777, page 13 of *Book Two*.

Dominance and Submission in Ritual

We're going to look at two rituals here: a dedication ceremony and a mild kink ritual. Both are pretty light, leaving lots of room for you to make it your own. Your ritual path and the nature of your group will shape one, and your kink preferences will shape the other.

One of the things we've done with ritual in these pages is make explicit a polarity that might already be implicit. For example, in the force/form ritual in chapter 7, I noted that force and form underlie the gender roles in Wicca. Normally, no one is stating "I am force" or "I am form," but in order to see the polarity for what it is and unhook it from gender essentialism, stating it explicitly is helpful. However, no other polarity is as consistently explicit as dominance and submission. Whether in kink, playing at master/slave, or at work, experiencing boss/employee, or indeed in religious rites, where the worshiper is submissive to the worshiped, the essential nature of the polarity is always spelled out. In fact, in kink, the nature and degree of dominance and submission are typically defined, discussed, and mutually agreed to before any ritual, scene, or action begins.

Dominance/Submission Ritual: Kink

Keep in mind that everyone's kink is individual. If it isn't going to turn you on, it's not an effective kink ritual, so my definition of a dominance/submission ritual may need to be modified for you. With that in mind, I've left a blank space in the middle of this ritual for you to explore dominance and submission as you see fit.

Also, people who participate in kink often already have some rituals, or at least ritualized behavior. This might include the use of honorifics or other keywords (the submissive calling the dominant "Sir," for example), other ritualized phrases, ritualized clothing, body positions, and ritualized actions. A common ritual in a D/S scene is for the submissive to bring the dominant their tools of dominance (floggers and what have you).

The point is, if this is something you do, you'll be adding some structures or ideas about energy work to your existing routine, not learning a new routine from me. To that end, the ritual I've created is simple and familiar in intent to many in the kink community. It is easily adapted to your own version of dominance and submission. It's also completely accessible to people who aren't a part of the kink community but want to explore this polarity energy.

In my book *Magical Power for Beginners,* I explore at length various ways of raising power. Many of these are sometimes a part of kinky D/S play, including pleasure, pain (potentially), consciousness alteration, and (again potentially) rhythm. Naturally, magical practitioners who are also kinky have noticed the inherent power in their kink and may have already explored its potential as an act of magic and/or worship. Harrington's excellent book *Sacred Kink* explores a variety of purposes to which kink energy can be directed, as well as the many ways to raise that energy. Polarity is an energy technique that can be added to the list.

The act of collaring is widely used in the kink community to ritualize and formalize a dominant/submissive relationship. Some people are in full-time BDSM relationships, often known as total power exchange (TPE). In this case, the submissive may wear a collar at all times. More typically, the dominant is the only one with control of the collar (the submissive may not don or remove it themselves), so putting on the collar formally begins the scene and removing it formally ends the scene. That is the ritual that we are performing here, with added visualization about polarity.

The collar itself can be anything: a piece of jewelry in the form of a lock, an actual chain with a padlock, a dog collar, a fancy piece of leather-work, a belt cut down to size, etc. Whatever it is, the dominant and the submissive agree in advance that this is the collar and that it symbolizes that the person placing/removing it is dominant and the person wearing it is submissive.

The couple agrees in advance to what the parameters of the dominance and submission will be: what is allowed, what is off-limits, what the expectations are, etc. Most kinky couples choose a safeword that can be used to stop all action. Traffic safewords, for example, are *red* for "stop," *yellow* for "slow down," *green* for "this is fine, go ahead," and perhaps *blue* for "everything is fine, but I need to explain something."

Note that the ritual begins with the dominant requesting that the submissive cede power—the request itself is an act of submission. The ability to say yes or no is an act of dominance.

Dominant: *Are you ready and willing to cede your power to me?*

Submissive: *I am.* (Visualizes their personal dominance flowing into Dominant.)

Dominant: (Placing collar around Submissive's neck) *You are now submissive to me and subject to my orders. What I say goes, and what I do, you accept.*

Now the agreed-upon activities occur, with the submissive wearing the collar. This can be sexual, pain-related (whipping, flogging, spanking), endurance-related (the dominant forcing the submissive to maintain difficult postures), bondage, etc.

There is no need for the activity to be specifically kinky. You might just go to the grocery store together, with the submissive collared and following the dominant's orders. The submissive does not take any independent action except as agreed to in advance by the dominant. Two things happen here. First, it's a safe way for non-kinky folks to explore the energy of being in this polarity relationship, and second, it might be very erotic. Other non-kink activities include doing housework or one partner bathing/washing the other (this one works either way—the dominant washes the submissive because the submissive is helpless and does not act independently, or the submissive washes the dominant as an act of service).

When you're done, the dominant removes the collar. This time the submissive does not give permission, because until the collar is removed, the submissive has no permission to give. The submissive can, of course, politely request that the collar be removed or politely request that it be kept on for a while longer.

Dominant: *I will now remove your collar and release you from submission. Thank you for the gift of your power.*

Submissive: *Thank you for holding my power and for returning it to me.*

Journal/Discussion Prompts

- If you're already kinky, did you notice anything different about rit-ualizing the polarity as opposed to your usual kink behavior?
- If you're not already kinky, did you enjoy this exploration? Did you find power in it?
- Do you find yourself drawn to the dominant or submissive role, or both? Why?
- The liminal space between dominant and submission is equity. Did you notice or experience moments of equity in this ritual? What was that like?

Dominance/Submission Ritual: Dedication

This is a tricky ritual to present here, because if you are a member of a p-word group, you either already have a dedication or initiation ceremony or you purposely eschew having one. It's additionally tricky because the mutually-agreed-upon energy flow used in a polarity working might in some ways be at odds with the very nature of letting an outsider in—you might not be figuring out the structure of working energy together until after you're *all* inside.

But I'm boldly moving ahead with some reasonable limitations. First, this is a dedication to studying with a group, not initiation into an inner circle. (I know nothing about what *your* inner circle has going on.) Second, the polarity of dominance and submission is spelled out carefully in the ritual so that the dedicant is clued in.

The dedicant is the submissive here, and the dominant will be called "leader." Normally, a guide (a second member of the group) is helpful in such rituals to bring the dedicant in at the right time and prompt them if they forget what to do. The dedicant has been given instructions in advance regardless (at least in order to make the wand).

YOU'LL NEED

- An altar, about coffee-table height
- Any other symbols of your group that belong on the altar, such as deity symbols

- A wand prepared by the dedicant in advance of the ritual
- Cords for binding the dedicant
- A spear or sword to be used by the leader
- A bell

Your ritual space is prepared in accordance with your normal steps. The dedicant waits outside the space. A bell signals the dedicant to come to the edge of the space.

Leader: *Are you ready to dedicate yourself to [name of group] and its ways?*

Dedicant: *I am.*

Leader: *Then for this rite of dedication, you must cede your power to [name of group]. Do you give over this power willingly?*

Dedicant: *I do.*

Leader: (Points sword or spear at dedicant) *Then I command you give over a symbol of your dedication, that your power may flow through it to us* (Places sword/spear on the altar).

Dedicant: (Hands wand to the leader while both visualize the flow of power)

Leader: (Binds dedicant's hands behind their back with cords, then leads dedicant three times around the ritual space, ending at the altar. Leader rings bell three times, then assists dedicant into a kneeling position, placing their head on the altar. Leader picks up sword/spear and again points it at the dedicant.)

Repeat after me. I [name of dedicant], do hereby swear…

Dedicant: (Repeats words)

Leader: *To be honest and forthright with [name of group]…*

Dedicant: (Repeats words)

Leader: *To be devoted in my studies…*

Dedicant: (Repeats words)

Leader: *And to be loyal to the gods.*

Dedicant: (Repeats words)

Leader: *So be it!*

Dedicant: (Repeats words)

Leader: (Returns sword/spear to altar and rings bell three times. Assists dedicant to rise and removes cords.)

As your power has been given to us, so we now return it to you. (Hands wand back to dedicant.) *We welcome you now as an equal.* (The two embrace.)

Journal/Discussion Prompts

- What was the experience of this ritual like? If you were the leader, did the dedicant also share their experience?
- How might this ritual be modified for a solitary practitioner? How would the power flow in a solitary ritual?

Chapter Eleven

Night and Day

Night and day add two unique aspects to polarity that we haven't previously discussed. First, they are nature-based without being about fertility; this is a natural polarity that doesn't procreate humans, animals, or plants. It just *is*. Second, night and day contain and flow into each other. *Dawn* and *twilight* are, to me, the very epitome of liminality. They don't divide; they cycle.

When we talk about dominance and submission containing each other, we still see clear dividing lines. *Here* is where I have power and *here* is where I cede power. But I have sat and watched a sunset and still somehow been surprised to look up and find it full dark. Night, like the fog, comes on little cat feet, creeping up bit by bit. Automatic light sensors turn streetlights on and off, and each time I am just a bit surprised because each time I am immersed in the transition, feeling day (or night) flowing toward night (or day) and not realizing it has fully departed.

Night and day are a dance of ebb and flow. While in chapter 9 we talked about the passive/active polarity of being/becoming, here night is continually becoming day and day is continually becoming night. When is night just "being" night? At the stroke of midnight? Isn't it holding the potentiality, indeed the inevitability, of day even then?

Yet daylight and nighttime are also uniquely themselves. Day brings brightness, sunlight, wakefulness, and diurnal creatures; birdsong and all manner of animal sounds in nature; as well as lively city sounds of horns and traffic and people. Night brings secrecy and mystery, indirect lighting, sleep or sleeplessness, hooting owls, and a whole different set of human and animal sounds. We know, and can sense, the distinct differences, the way that plants seek the sun and slumber at night, the feeling of dew in the morning and the sultry aura of evening.

The Third

We have already mentioned liminality. The "third" between night and day is twilight or dawn. Indeed, the ebb-and-flow nature of the polarity of night and day means that part of their very essence is the ongoing presence of the space between them.

Liminality is meaningful to human beings who don't fit into neat categories (including queer people, people of mixed race, intersex and nonbinary people, and people with multiple nationalities), and it is meaningful to magic. A liminal space can be a void into which you can step, in which rules do not apply. The Lord of Misrule governs the space that is neither the old year nor the new year, because in between, misrule *is* the rule. Where there are no rules, we make our own rules, and this is powerful magic indeed. This is why, for example, there is a tradition of doing magic at the crossroads—it is neither the north-south road nor the east-west road, but a space betwixt and between. This in-between space is nonlinear, so "impossible" things can be made to happen here.

Going to a crossroads is one way to create liminal space for magic, as is choosing a "void" time on the calendar (such as the time between Yule and New Year, which is when the Lord of Misrule has sway). In Wicca, the magic circle is considered a "world between the worlds" and is inherently a liminal space. Another way to create this space is by finding the betwixt-and-between spot in a polarity. Remember, *sublimation and contrast.* By keeping the poles far apart and *then* bringing them together (sublimation), the space of their intersection is created with a *bang.* On the other hand, by continually moving a ritual back and forth between the two (contrast), the liminal space builds gradually, like filling a bucket. Day and night polarity allows for a third possibility: that the liminal space already exists; it simply *is*. It can be honored as itself in ritual and brought to bear for magical purposes.

The third here is also the full twenty-four-hour cycle. The endless repetition and cycling can be empowering or maddening. Maybe because I work really hard, I have a tendency to see a twenty-four-hour cycle as a hamster wheel, a ceaseless grind without respite. But it is also a completion, a fullness, and a continuity.

As with not seeing clearly the moment that dawn becomes day, we don't see clearly the moment that yesterday becomes today (except by using a clock or other device). So the fullness of a day cycle is a hint of eternity. That day cycle is also a month cycle, also a year cycle, also a lifetime.

Other Polarities That Are Night/Day

It is obvious that **sun and moon** are cognate to day and night. Are they polar? Not as celestial objects, certainly, but as fixed points within the ever-moving polarity of day and night, yes. What I mean is I have described day and night as continually flowing into one another, and containing one another, and I have stated that even midnight does not define a fixed point of night. However, the moon *does* represent that fixed point. It is a physical object, and while the object itself is not a "pole," its existence communicates the solidity of the pole. Thus, it allows you to stop at a moment of night, say *this is the pole*, and turn and look toward the day/sun. Sun and moon as a polarity are also useful in finding deities of these poles, as sun and moon deities are prevalent throughout the world—day and night deities less so.

While we're being sun/moon binary, let's pause to note that sometimes the moon is visible during daylight, and, fundamentally, the sun is almost always "visible" at night—in the reflection that is moonlight. Even on a cloudy night when the moon is not visible, any ambient light allowing you to see at night is, indirectly, sunlight.

Earth and sky also comprise a nature-based polarity that isn't directly procreative. Agriculturally, we can see that sky nurtures earth, providing sunshine, rain, and wind (which spreads pollen and seeds). However, the fertilization has already happened within the earth; the seed is already planted without the participation of the sky (wind transports some seeds, but the earth does all the work). Earth and sky are also cyclical—rain falls from the sky onto the earth, where it evaporates back to the sky. Earth and sky, like day and night, are dancing together, recycling into each other, and meeting at the horizon.

Winter and summer, as the times of year when light is shortest/longest, are another form of day/night polarity, with the solstices being the extremes of each pole and the equinoxes their liminal state of balance.

Yin and yang contain each other, as we've seen. Like night and day, one appears dark but contains light, while one appears light but contains dark. Valiente likens yin and yang to Chokmah and Binah, as well as **Jachin and Boaz** (the pillars of King Solomon's Temple in Freemasonry), and the "alchemical symbolism [of] the masculine sun and the feminine moon."[149]

Since we've identified day/night as a polarity of ebb and flow, we can include **high tide and low tide** as a kind of polarity that illustrates that ebb and flow in the natural world. Here's a case where there is a clear and identifiable point—in the waterline, high tide is visible to the naked eye even after it has passed. Low tide is less visible to the casual observer (the line is underwater, after all), but to someone who knows that particular piece of shore well, it's obvious. Despite that, the tides are characterized by constant movement; the moment of high or low tide doesn't hold still or isolate itself from its other pole.

Since we're talking about tides, the next obvious pole is that of the **waxing moon and waning moon.** I love ideas that contain each other like nesting dolls. Just a moment ago, we identified sun/moon as a polarity, and now it's moon/moon. In my book *The Way of Four*, I divide lots and lots of things by the four elements. Yet repeatedly, we find that there's a kind of nesting, a fractal repetition, of elements within elements.

---

149. Valiente, *Witchcraft for Tomorrow*, 28.

For example, in a person we can say that Air is mind, Fire is spirit, Water is heart/emotion, and Earth is body. But we can also take the concept of "body" and say that Air is the respiratory system, Water is the circulatory and lymphatic systems, Fire is the nervous system, and Earth is muscle, fat, bone, and sinew. Similarly, it's clear that Water corresponds to liquids generally. Yet we can take the idea of "beverage" and divide it into Air (carbonated drinks, as well as saki, since rice is associated with Air), Fire (alcoholic spirits), Water (water itself, as well as wine and anything sweet or syrupy), and Earth (beer and milk).

When we transfer this idea from four to two, from elements to polarities, the notion of polarities within polarities is not just a fun game; it's an important teaching about the nature of polarity. A traditional yin/yang symbol is black and white. But the relationship remains relative. Leave the white yang as is and change the yin to light gray. Their polarity hasn't changed, but the separation of the poles has. But now leave the yin that same gray and make the yang a darker gray. Now the polarity has reversed *for that example*. Light gray is now "yin" to white but "yang" to dark gray.

Relative Polarity in Yin/Yang

Moon is still "night" to the sun, but waxing and waning is its own polarity, and the polar position of "moon" is now relative.

Another pair of seeming opposites that bleed into each other is **dreaming and waking.** In a polarity of consciousness, these are two extremes, but most of us have had the experience of a "waking dream" state, where wakefulness seems unreal, and we've all had dreams that we were sure were real. In training yourself to have lucid dreams, one technique is to ask yourself continually, while awake, "Am I awake or is this a dream?" This gets you in the habit of asking the question and looking for evidence, so that you'll do the same when asleep. The exercise is fascinating and I recommend it even if you don't end up being a skilled lucid dreamer (I didn't). One time a city bus passed me by, and the distinctive odor of bus exhaust overwhelmed me. I asked myself if I was dreaming and I answered, "No, I don't think I have a sense of smell in my dreams. I'm awake." I completely missed the fact that the bus was *in my living room*. Distinguishing between dreams and wakefulness is tricky!

By the way, if you wish to explore the polarity of dreaming/waking, I recommend *Lucid Dreams in 30 Days* by Keith Harary and Pamela Weintraub, the book I used for the training above. These "30 days" programs are more rigid than I'm capable of, and a few exercises I repeated several times before I was satisfied with them. Nevertheless, in 40 or 45 days I learned an enormous amount about my own consciousness and how I shift between these states, and I had a few mild successes with lucid dreaming.

Finally, and most profoundly, we can look at the polarity of **death and rebirth.** It is often said that death is a kind of sleep and that dying is merely a change in consciousness when consciousness is no longer housed in the body. Masters of many traditions liken death to a dream state, or even liken *life* to a dream, housed in the body, while death is the full awakening of the spirit without the dreamlike interference of bodily awareness.

If you don't believe in reincarnation or resurrection, you can argue that life and death are purely separate poles, with a clear dividing line. But even then, there are near-death experiences and liminal states between life and death. I have a friend who is a nurse. Her professional experience began at a nursing home where she was often called upon to sit with dying patients in their final moments. Her subsequent career has included working at an abortion clinic, working in labor and delivery, and working in a hospital for criminal psychiatric patients. Each of these is a liminal state; the last one a liminal state of consciousness, the others all between life and death. Her entire career has existed in this particular polarity space.

Death and rebirth is not necessarily a polarity you'd want to work with often, and certainly not one you'll embody literally, but it can be an awakening experience to understand its relationship to other polarities of this group, which you experience more directly.

Deities of Day and Night

Western magic would have you believe that the moon is female, the sun is male, and never the twain shall meet. This gender assignment is certainly true throughout Western magic, and goes back for millennia. However, it is anything but universal. Indeed, it's probably true that if you took every culture worldwide and looked at their mythology, the gender of sun and moon would be distributed just about randomly. Sun and moon might be male/female, female/male, female/female, or male/male in just about equal proportions.

In Egyptian myth, **Ra** is the god of both the sun and the day. **Nuit** is the goddess of night, and **Khonsu** is the god of the moon. The goddess **Nephthys** is the twilight, and the goddess **Tefnut** is the dawn.

In Hinduism, the god **Surya** embodies the sun, much the way Ra does in Egypt or **Helios** does in Greece. The goddess of light is **Aditi,** and solar deities as a group are called **Adityas** (Aditya as a singular is another name for Surya). The goddess **Lakshmi** is the primary goddess worshiped at Diwali, the festival of light. **Ushas** is the Vedic goddess of the dawn, and her sister, **Ratri,** is the night. In addition, **Chandra** is the god of the moon, while **Shiva** carries the moon on his head.

In Greek myth, Helios embodies the sun, while **Apollo** is its ruler. The triple goddess of the moon is **Artemis** for the waxing moon, **Selene** for the full moon, and **Hecate** for the waning and dark moon. **Eos** is the goddess of dawn. **Nyx** is the goddess of night, and her daughters, the **Hesperides,** are twilight.

This is by no means comprehensive. Day and night, sun and moon, and dawn and twilight give us some of the richest mythologies from which to choose, and I haven't even gotten into death and rebirth or dreams and waking!

As a polytheist, I take deity seriously, and I am not offering these names in the spirit of "plug and play." I don't much care for the idea of pulling a name from a list and cavalierly dropping it into a ritual slot. Rather, these names are meant as a source of exploration, a particularly rich source in the case of day/night polarity and its cognates.

In Kabbalah, the sixth sephirah, **Tiferet**, is associated with both the sun and resurrection, while the ninth sephirah, **Yesod**, is associated with the moon and with dream states. It is the sephirah associated with the very idea of liminality. It is also fitting that in a polarity focused heavily on the between-state, the corresponding sephirot are both on the middle pillar.

Day and Night in Humanity

In our relationships, one of the things that can be lacking is the sense that we are part of a single thing. Partnerships, family units, and even businesses are entities unto themselves, not just a bunch of component members. In marriage, for example, it's easy to look at yourself and your spouse as day and night, but it's healthy to remember that the marriage is its own being. I know that if I'm having a particularly bad day/week/month, if I'm moody or miserable, or if the news of the day is triggering my worst terrors, I might treat others in my life badly. At those times, it's helpful to recognize that *me* is the problem, not *us*. In the metaphor of "day and night," the sky's dark time is a problem, not the sky itself. This too, as they say, shall pass.

Day and night polarity can remind us of two important things: first, that the twenty-four-hour cycle of a full day requires both, and second, that we aren't as different as we appear.

People love to joke about the "opposites attract" aspect of any couple. While the fact is that people who marry each other tend to have far more in common than not, it's also true that two people who *both* want to sleep with the windows open never seem to get together, and we all joke about that. But the idea that you're day and I'm night is illusory, and sometimes it's harmful. We can reconnect with each other only if we remember that we're both dawn and twilight, and we're both fully rounded humans, not just the other person's "other half."

When we remember that, then the difference can be playful and, yes, humorous and enlivening.

Both day and night are necessary in order to fill the sky. On the job, my work involves functioning as a liaison between clients on the one side and software developers on the other. I communicate the client's needs to the techies and take the results back to the clients. It's interactive and it suits me. Sometimes understanding the client takes a bit of telepathy, and sometimes working with them requires a bit of social work. I use my "soft skills," my ability to communicate and understand, often. Then I take the requirements back to the techies, and they're rigid and don't communicate well, and they don't see the big picture. It can be infuriating, up until the point when I remember there's a reason that a team needs one of them *and* one of me. If I had those tech skills, well, I'd have that job (they tend to earn more). The ability to do that kind of technical work goes hand-in-hand with seeing more trees than forest, while the ability to do what I do is served by seeing the forest more than the trees. Instead of getting annoyed with the software developers for the very character traits I lack, I can appreciate how much the team needs people like them as well as people like me; together we comprise the whole sky.

Magical Tools of Day and Night

Some traditions use a cross or rose cross to represent rebirth. Some traditions use an ankh, symbolizing rebirth, renewal, and the joining of polarities (including sexual joining[150]), and these are appropriate tools. Some traditions have specific solar and lunar symbols, such as moon and sun crowns. Crowley gives "the Lamen or Rosy Cross" for Tiferet and "the Perfumes and Sandals" for Yesod.

Day and Night in Ritual

In exploring rituals of polarity, we have some choices. I can offer a ritual in which a polarity is already present, and dig into the way that manifests.

---

150. The circular part represents the yoni—the vulva—and the long arm represents the phallus. The crosspiece is their joining.

We can accentuate the way that a polarity is already present, dramatizing it, so that the ritual illuminates for us the way that we function in relation to that polarity, what it feels like, and what it means to us. We can also have the ritual be *about* that polarity, saying, essentially, here it is: here's a ritual of day and night (or something else). We've been doing a bit of each so far in this volume.

Occult and Pagan rituals are replete with day and night as a polarity or as a direct experience. There are lunar rituals, solar rituals, rituals of the turning year, of the dawn, of midnight, and on and on. Both the Christian and Jewish calendars time celebrations by the sun and moon, as do many native traditions worldwide. So, for day and night, it seems redundant to offer a ritual in which it's already present: Here's another full moon rite, as if there weren't already a dozen books on your shelf containing exactly that. The exploration of sun and moon seems almost like a cliché.

Instead, we're going to look at a couple of "here it is" rituals in which the whole point of the rite is to explore this particular polarity. We'll be manifesting day and night as people, using sun and moon symbols to express day and night succinctly. Below are a ritual for a couple and a ritual for a group. Both rituals use movement to explore the interaction of the poles.

Some points to note:

- Adapt freely to work within any mobility limits you may have. This can be done as a slow dance (as written), seated with just arms moving, or in any way that is comfortable and accessible for you.

- Movement benefits from music, so you might want to have recorded music that suits the mood, or someone might drum to maintain a rhythm.

- For movement rituals, it is important that the space is clear of obstructions. If indoors, check for things like loose corners of carpeting. For outdoor rituals, do a walk-through looking for holes, stones, and other potential hazards.

- If working outdoors, explore how the time of day or night might impact the ritual. Perhaps you might perform it once in darkness and then another time in light. Similarly, ask how the time of year or the moon phase might have impacted your experience.

- These rituals ask you to have solar and lunar symbols that can be worn. They should be easily removed and replaced. I like pendants, which can be as simple as suns and moons made of card stock and strung onto yarn. You could also use stickers, brightly colored scarves, headbands, etc.

- You'll need four solar symbols and four lunar symbols per person in each ritual.

Each ritual depends heavily on your ability to visualize and experience the polar energies in yourself and the other participant(s). It's important, then, to begin with meditation, grounding, or whatever techniques you use to enhance your sensitivity to the moment and to energy.

The Day/Night Couple Ritual

The purpose of this ritual is to embody a polarity, sense it, sense its opposite pole in your partner, and experience the movement of polar energy between partners.

For the day/night couple ritual, decide in advance who will be day and who will be night. Perhaps you are an opposite-sex couple and want to use the traditional Western gender polarity of male/day and female/night. Perhaps each of you is naturally drawn more toward one or the other. Perhaps you'll choose by a different means entirely. It's up to you. (There's nothing stopping you from doing the ritual a second time so that each of you can experience each role.) When you listen to the meditation below, do it from the point of view of whichever pole you have chosen.

After your grounding or other opening meditation or exercise, begin by putting on the symbols of your time of day. The day partner wears four sun or day symbols. The night partner wears four moon or night symbols.

When you are ready, use the following meditation. It's ideal to record it
and play it back during ritual so that you can experience it together.

*Close your eyes and take a deep cleansing breath. Breathe in through
your nose, hold, let it out through your mouth. Breathe in, hold, let it out.
Breathe in, hold, let it out.*

*It is dawn. The sky grows light. Breathe in the light. Do you breathe
in yourself, becoming more you as the light grows? Or is this your time of
fading? Either way, feel the light coming, and know the light. What does
light and dawn feel like?*

*The day grows. Light increases. It's a hot, sunny day, the sky is blue,
and you hear birds. Is this your time or the time of your partner? Feel its
energy, its heat, and listen to its music.*

*The day moves toward its end. Sunset approaches. Look at the late
afternoon sky. What does the air feel like? What do you experience as day
begins to move toward evening?*

*It is now sunset. The sky is ablaze with color in the west. In the east,
the moon rises. Do you fade with the sun, or is the moonrise the rising of
your spirit? Feel the onset of darkness. Feel the coolness coming on.*

*Night deepens. You hear owls and nighttime creatures. Is this your time
or the time of your partner? Feel the energy of night, see the shadows, and
sense the quiet.*

*The night moves toward its wee hours. Dawn approaches. What does
the air feel like now? What do you experience as night begins to move
toward daylight?*

*As dawn approaches and the cycle begins again, allow yourself to
breathe deeply once more. You are day or night. You know yourself and
your energy, and you are ready to dance the dance of your time.*

Open your eyes.

Now the partners both stand facing each other. Bring your hands
together in front of your chest in namaste position. Feel yourself full of
the energy of your time, day or night. You are pulsing with day or night.

When recording, pause after each question is asked to give yourselves time to experience the answer during the meditation.

Hands in Namaste Position

Reach out so that your hands and your partner's hands nearly touch. Feel a back-and-forth pulse between day and night.

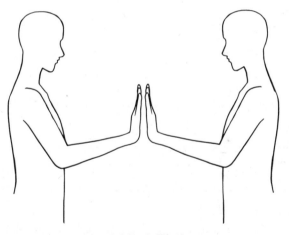

Hands Nearly Touching

When you are ready, slowly sway together, sensing each other's energy. Day pushes day energy gently to their partner. Night does the same, gently pushing the feeling of night. Perhaps you pull away from and toward each other in your dance.

When the moment feels right, one partner takes off one symbol and puts it on the other (that is, Day takes off a day necklace and puts it around Night's neck). The other partner responds by taking off one of their own necklaces and putting it on their partner. Each is now wearing symbols in a 3:1 proportion. Allow yourself to feel that—what is it like to have night sharing a bit of day, day sharing a bit of night? Feel the way your solar or lunar energy has taken on a bit of balance.

Continue to dance. When you're ready, trade necklaces again. Now you're each exactly even—split 2:2. Hold still—your energy in perfect balance momentarily does not move. Feel what that's like.

Continue to dance. The partner who was Day will give up another sun symbol, and the partner who was Night will give up another moon symbol, so that now each is dominated by their "opposite" energy. Dance with that and feel what it's like.

Dance toward a final exchange of symbols so that Day wears 100 percent night and vice versa. What does it feel like to have shifted polarities completely in the course of this dance?

Ground and center again.

The Day/Night Group Ritual

The purpose of this ritual is to discover your own relationship to a polarity, and to experience it in relation to the polarities of others.

For the day/night group ritual, you will choose your polarity alignment after (as a result of) the meditation. Since there are four day and four night symbols available per person, anyone can choose any combination of four symbols after the meditation ends, allowing for the presence of a full range of day/night expressions.

Begin with your grounding or other opening meditation or exercise and then declare a purpose. Discuss the ritual and its steps so that everyone knows what's expected of them. Make sure each participant has a set of eight symbols available in front of them.

When you are ready, use the following meditation. It can be recorded and played back, or one person can choose to be reader and guide. When recording, or when the guide is reciting, pause after each question is asked to give yourselves time to experience the answer during the meditation.

Close your eyes and take a deep cleansing breath. Breathe in through your nose, hold, let it out through your mouth. Breathe in, hold, let it out. Breathe in, hold, let it out.

It is dawn. The sky grows light. Breathe in the light. What is the nature of this moment, of dark fading and day breaking? Is this your energy? Feel the light coming, and know the light. What do light and dawn feel like? Feel the light within yourself and the light of dawn. Do you breathe in yourself, becoming more yourself as the light grows? Or is this your time of fading? Or do parts of you respond one way and parts respond another?

The day grows. Light increases. It's a hot, sunny day, the sky is blue, and you hear birds. Feel the day, its energy and its heat, and listen to its music. Feel the brightness of this moment. Does a brightness within you respond? Does a darkness within you shrink away?

The day moves toward its end. Sunset approaches. Look at the late afternoon sky. What does the air feel like? What do you experience as day begins to move toward evening?

It is now sunset. The sky is ablaze with color in the west. In the east, the moon rises. Do you fade with the sun, or is the moonrise the rising of your spirit? Perhaps you feel both at once. Allow yourself to experience the onset of darkness. Feel the coolness coming on.

Night deepens. You hear owls and nighttime creatures. Feel the energy of night, see the shadows, and sense the quiet. Do you come alive to the night sounds? Do you feel fully yourself? Does a part of you, or all of you, disappear when the sun is gone? Feel yourself as a part of night and understand that it is yours, or not yours.

The night moves toward its wee hours. Dawn approaches. What does the air feel like now? What do you experience as night begins to move toward daylight?

As dawn approaches and the cycle begins again, allow yourself to breathe deeply once more. You are day or night, or both, in some measure. You know yourself and your energy, and you are ready to dance the dance of your time.

Open your eyes. See before you a set of symbols. Choose the symbols that belong to you and put them around your neck.[151]

Did you come to know that you are fully a person of day? Choose four sun symbols.

Did you come to know that you are fully a person of night? Choose four moon symbols.

Did you come to know that you are a person of day, with night a part of you? Choose three sun symbols and one moon symbol.

Did you come to know that you are a person of night, with day a part of you? Choose three moon symbols and one sun symbol.

Did you come to know that you are equally divided between night and day energies? Choose two of each symbol.

Wearing your symbols, stand up and move around the circle. Notice other people's symbols. Notice who you want to dance with, whose energy is opposite yours or like yours. If you are equally divided, you may choose to stand still to represent the balance point. Let others come to you.

One at a time, each person (beginning with a leader, which will remind everyone that this had been part of the instructions) will make a brief statement about themselves, like "I am sun/moon" or "I am the bright noon" or "I am twilight"—whatever they like.

The ritual is now free-form. Participants will move silently around the ritual space (perhaps accompanied by music or drumming), exploring their own energies in connection with others. Alternatively, people can all continue to chant their statement as a kind of mantra, walking or dancing while saying/chanting "I am the bright noon" while others chant their own day/night mantra.

People can seek their opposites (for example, three suns and a moon finding three moons and a sun) for a polar dance, or they might simply use hands and movement to feel the energies shift as they move around the room.

---

151. Put them around your neck if they are pendants. Change this language if you are using a different kind of symbol.

If people are moved to trade symbols, they can do so, but the exchange of energies is not the point of this ritual.

The ritual should end with a grounding activity such as eating bread.

Journal/Discussion Prompts

- Do you have a feeling that you are certain of your day/night polarity? Of what it "is"?
- Do you relate that feeling to gender in any way?
- What is the day in your night? The night in your day?
- What was it like to choose your day/night polarity?
- What was it like to experience your polarity being shifted?
- What was it like to shift the polarity of your partner?
- Can you describe the experience of each "level" of polarity? Of 4:0, of 3:1, of 2:2?

Chapter Twelve

Gender Polarities

In chapter 5 we discussed the Great Work of alchemy. The process of breaking something apart, purifying it, and bringing it back together is known as *solve et coagula*, dissolve and unite (or coagulate).

We can't know a thing until we take it apart and look at the pieces. We can't know cake until we look at milk, flour, and eggs. We can't know eggs until we look at shell, albumin, and yolk. Alchemy takes each component and purifies it, making it holy. That which cannot be made holy is discarded. The final step is bringing all the purified components back together.

We've dissolved polarity in these pages. We've taken apart its components, seen their sacredness, and examined their necessary and unnecessary parts. Now we're ready for *coagula*, for putting these pieces back together, and including gender in the mix. We could have talked about gender like any other polarity, of course. But with gender comes a ton of cultural baggage, including within the magical community; so we needed to explore other polarities and experience their energies, disconnected from gender, before it made sense to circle back. We started, after all, from the basis of so many traditions that say gender *is* polarity. Experiencing other polarities in the preceding chapters allows us to explore gender more freely, and more sanely.

On our journey through the history of polarity, we've seen a lot of things that have been described, symbolically or literally, as having gender. In alchemy, sulfur is "male" and mercury is "female," but this is purely a labeling system. By the time we get to the Golden Dawn, female *is* passive, and the woman magician is expected to embody that energy.

We've deconstructed that, polarity by polarity. We've seen force and form, passive and active, sun and moon, all manifest without gender, and we've explored, theoretically and ritually, how those energies work. Now we're ready to look at gender itself, without all the stuff attached to it over the centuries.

We've also seen that gender polarity means multiple things. Heteronormative culture has the privilege of conflating those things—morphology (body shape), gender identity, and sexual attraction. While a heterosexual couple can assume all three polarities exist at once, the rest of us have to approach gender polarity with more conscious consideration. For that reason, rather than do an "other polarities" section, as in the previous chapters, we'll be more expansive, giving each gender polarity its own section. I named this chapter "Gender *Polarities*" to emphasize that *gender polarity* is not a singular term and requires us to dive more deeply.

Gender Polarity of the Body

A lot of people say that "sex" is what your body is, and "gender" is what your head is (your gender identity). Scholars and theorists tend to disagree, understanding sex as a complex set of factors that includes gender identity. As we've seen, your body's sex isn't necessarily all that clear. Your chromosomes, your genitalia, and your secondary sex characteristics (things like breasts and beards that identify sex but are not genitals) don't necessarily align.

Let me clue you in to a little secret: No one cares about chromosomes. Some transphobic people have started to use the term "chromosomal sex/gender" because it sounds more scientific, and because they want to exclude trans people from inclusion in spaces where their body shape and genitalia more or less match the requirement (such as excluding trans women from women-only spaces). Transphobes don't care about your DNA; they care what's in your pants. But more than that, they care that they can continue to be bigots. So we won't be dealing with "chromosomal sex" here.

Interestingly, people respond more viscerally to secondary characteristics than to primary ones, probably because we don't go around checking out what's in people's pants on a day-to-day basis. I've been completely unable to find the study I read about some years ago and cannot footnote it, but here's a description: Basically, you show people illustrations of a person who looks very female—hourglass figure, "pretty" features, and so on—and of a person who looks very male—broad shoulders, beard, square jaw. You ask the participants to assign genders to the illustrations. Then you show the same two illustrations naked, so that the apparent woman is shown to have a penis and the apparent man is shown to have a vulva. You ask the same people to assign gender to the new illustrations. Most people will stick with their original assumptions—the woman with a penis is still a woman. People who "seem like" men or women are perceived as, and treated as, men and women, and this is regardless of any preconceptions a person might have about trans or queer people.

As we've discussed, traditional polarity systems of the past century or so assume that gendered bodies generate polarity just by being. That is, if there are both men and women present (however that is defined), that's enough to generate polarity.

I want to be 100 percent clear that polarity based on gendered bodies works. It is usually an uncomfortable way of being polar for genderqueer, nonbinary, and trans people, but if no such people are present and/or everyone is comfortable, this is a time-honored and effective way of generating polarity energy. It naturally works best when ritual acts emphasize the polarity, using sublimation or contrast to continually underline the presence of gendered bodies. Maybe it works based on pheromones, maybe by some other biological trait, maybe it's the placebo effect—it works because people think it will work. But it definitely *does* work. I've been saying from the beginning there's a baby in this bathwater, and there's a reason that people want to hold onto polarity as a magical tool. If this kind of body polarity is your favorite, and no occultists are harmed in the making of this ritual, there's no reason not to use it.

On the other hand, if you're using biological gender polarity all the time, you might be subconsciously avoiding adding people for whom it doesn't work to your group. You might also be inhibiting people in your group from exploring their own gender identity deeply or from coming out. Tread carefully in these waters. As discussed in chapter 10, a group with a boundary between in and out has dominance over a person who wishes to be in. The inherent power of any group might cause a gender-normative group to be—even inadvertently—imposing gender norms on all its members. This isn't hypothetical. I know at least one queer person whose coming out was complicated by fear of losing a tradition they loved.

Polarity of Gender Identity or Gender Expression

Polarities of gender identity and gender expression work the same way as polarities of the body but allow each individual the freedom to define for themselves what their gender pole is.

When I say "identity," I mean how you define yourself. A trans woman defines herself as a woman. Both out of respect for every human's inner wisdom (a core principle of most p-word theologies) and because current science indicates that trans people are, in fact, correct in their perception of their gender (at least according to brain function[152]), self-identity *is* identity and can be treated ritually as "real."

For most people, gender identity, like orientation, isn't a choice—I didn't choose to be a cis woman, I was born that way. But the terminology used as part of self-definition, especially in our current state of linguistic flux, definitely is a choice, and as people do the inner work of discovering their authentic selves, respecting their language is important.

A note about "identity." I identify myself as a cisgender woman. My daughter identifies herself as a transgender woman. But watch out for using

---

152. European Society of Endocrinology. "Transgender Brains Are More Like Their Desired Gender from an Early Age."

"identify as" to subtly imply that identity is other than reality. If you say I "am" a woman but my daughter "identifies as" a woman, I'm going to say that's a microaggression; that you're treating her identity as less "woman" than mine.

What does any of this mean for how nonbinary people might function in a ritual space where gender polarity is being leveraged, where that polarity is based on gender identity? What if your identity is neither/nor? Or both/and?

What I offer here is intended as a conversation, not as instruction. I know what works for the nonbinary people I know and do ritual with, but they are not, and cannot be, representative of all nonbinary people. If my suggestions or ideas here don't work for you, throw them away. Remember, there are lots of polarities to explore other than gender polarities, and it might be that this entire area is one where potential power is complicated too much by your life history, by oppression you've experienced, or simply by your unique self. I hope my thoughts here have value for you, but if they don't, feel free to discard them.

Remember that polarity doesn't necessarily mean that everyone and everything is one pole or the other. Just as a black/white polarity implies the existence of every shade of gray, gender polarity implies a range of genders between polar male and polar female. If this is true for your gender identity or those you share ritual space with, then rituals can be designed with those liminal gray areas in mind. Many nonbinary identities exist neatly within polarity when we open our eyes to see it. A genderfluid person, for example, might experience themselves as moving along a pole, sometimes more male, sometimes more female. A friend described it to me as being like checking the weather before going out: "Today I'm cloudy with a chance of female."

Some nonbinary identities, though, don't fit on a pole at all. Even when we understand gender as a rainbow rather than a neat journey from black to white and back again, for some people it's more like a soup, all mixed together, male and female and no gender and all genders without any linearity. For such people, being required to fit on a pole, even a nuanced pole, can feel oppressive. They've been told all their lives to be one or the other, and it can hurt. Again, if that's you, any suggestion to work along the pole can be discarded entirely in regard to gender. Force and form, passive and active, etc., are all available to you without ever being trapped in a gender box.

Some nonbinary people do find a way to work with gender polarity that is deeply meaningful. "Expression" as a gender polarity allows people who may or may not identify as a gender, or as just one gender, to work with an aspect of gender that makes sense to them. My beloved Professor Spouse is nonbinary and identifies as butch. She is most comfortable in rituals (and otherwise) when she has a masculine gender expression. I have also encountered several nonbinary people whose gender expression in ritual doesn't necessarily align with their gender expression in day-to-day life, including nonbinary people who are binary in ritual, and binary people who are gender fluid in ritual.

Some nonbinary people I know have a fixed ritual gender that may or may not match their day-to-day gender. Professor Spouse is male in ritual, period. Others choose their gender per ritual, as in "Today I am a Priestess" or "Today I am a Priest." I have found this an effective and powerful means of honoring the person and the ritual's traditional polarity. In such rituals, where nonbinary people enact gender identity roles, I've found that the body quickly becomes invisible, and the expression is what you see. The male-identified woman with the hourglass figure reads clearly as "male," and the bearded bear expressing a feminine identity reads as "female." Energy is fun that way.

One thing that makes this easier is to have some kind of gender-designated symbol—a piece of jewelry worn only by women, for example. In that way, you can be a woman or man for purposes of ritual by donning or removing the woman-crown or woman-necklace. There are two kinds of Sneetches, and you have a star-belly or not.

Again, not everyone is comfortable with choosing a gender in this way. As one friend said to me, "Sometimes I feel female or male, but sometimes I'm more like a swarm of bees." If gender expression isn't something a particular nonbinary person does or wants to do, this whole ritual approach won't work. If the option makes sense to you, enjoy it, but please don't feel like it's the only way to be nonbinary in a polarity rite.

It's also noteworthy that you can find your own gender polarities in relation to a specific partner. One way to define polarity for Professor Spouse and me is as "male and female," since she functions as the masculine side of the spectrum and I function as the feminine. But another way we define ourselves is "butch and femme." Butch/femme identity is its own thing, its own unique gender expression with its own energy (as well as a long cultural history). As mentioned in chapter 10, "top and bottom" is one way that some couples—especially same-sex couples—identify the "gender" polarity of their relationship. (I should be clear that butch/femme is just one way that lesbian couples interact; many other lesbian couples don't experience or express a gender polarity. I should be *further* clear that I am using the word *lesbian* to modify *couples*—that is, a *lesbian couple* is a couple comprised of two women, regardless of the orientation of either.)

In the day/night group ritual at the end of chapter 11, you found your unique blend of day/night, and found its energetic connection to other such blends. You can do the same thing with gender, finding your own space/relationship with gender and exploring how that might connect in a polar way with a partner. Maybe it doesn't—but it's a powerful exploration.

Polarities of Lust and Love

Since people lump sex and gender together, it made sense to include sexual energy polarity here. Even though sexuality isn't necessarily tied to gender, it's rooted in the body and bodily experience and leverages the fact that our bodies have these cool genitals that can make us feel very good.

Just as gender identity may not work as a polarity for some nonbinary people, lust may not work magically for some asexual people, and love may not work for aromantic people. Fortunately, the polarity menu has lots of options other than these.

In chapter 3 we established that polarity is not originally rooted in sex—the *hieros gamos* is not particularly a polarity ritual. Nonetheless, part of polarity energy is *longing*. The electron is attracted to the proton and rushes toward it. The poles here are analogous to subject/object—the subject being the one who is attracted and the object being the one who is rushed toward. In this attraction, we can see desire, yearning, even passion. The difference is that we assume that each lover is both subject and object, both desirous and desired. (Otherwise it's less fun.)

Remember that polarity energy is generated by the act of yearning toward the opposite pole. The magic of orgasm is magic indeed, but the polarity part is in the act of moving *toward* sexual fulfillment, not achieving it. The polarity energy then gets layered into the sexual energy.

The Sexual Polarity Circuit

As we learned when discussing electricity in chapter 1, when a circuit is completed—by electrons reaching protons—it is grounded, and when it is interrupted or intercepted by something, that "something" can be powered by the circuit.

In a sexual polarity circuit, grounding is satisfaction, but also deep emotional connection. Grounding takes the energies of each partner, blends them, and interconnects them. This grounding can occur whether or not a magical goal is placed within the circuit to receive its energy, although when you have a magical goal, your focus is there and not on your relationship.

As mentioned in chapter 6, Dion Fortune had the idea that a same-sex couple could work extraordinarily powerful magic without ever needing to ground:

> Two streams of force of the same type are called forth, and naturally find no channels of return, as the vehicles are both of the same polarity. These forces are therefore available for magical purposes; hence the extensive use of what are commonly called obscene practices as one of the easiest ways of obtaining power.... The person so experimenting shall give himself over unreservedly to evil.[153]

---

153. Fortune, *The Esoteric Philosophy of Love and Marriage*, 96.

Obviously, Fortune was wrong about the evil. She was also wrong about the grounding. That's just not how sex works. In same-sex relationships, the polar circuit of desire is completed and the energy is grounded, sent forth into pleasure, into the relationship, toward magic, or to the gods, as the couple chooses. Without highly disciplined tantric practices, it's nearly impossible to have sex, or sex magic, *without* grounding the circuit.

The magical/psychic/emotional polar circuit can be created any number of ways; bodies are nearly infinite in the variety of ways available to raise pleasurable energy. One traditional way is through penetrative, face-to-face sex, which allows for both physical sexual connection and eye contact.

Penetrative polarity can be generated by any two people with a mind to it. If no one has a vagina, there are other things to penetrate. If no one has a penis, the magic works very well with a store-bought aid, or you can use your hand. In the description below, I'm assuming a face-to-face position that allows for eye contact and/or kissing, so unless you're very flexible, I'm not seeing a hand as ideal. This description assumes a man with a penis and a woman with a vagina, just for ease of sentence structure.

In heterosexual intercourse, it is typical, to the point of cliché, for the man to thrust all his psychic energy into his partner at the moment of orgasm. If no one is paying attention to energy, the result is that the man, spent, falls immediately asleep, while the woman is hyped up. I used to say, "You go to sleep, dear, I'll just be feather-dusting the roof." Instead, you can be conscious of the energy and create a circuit.

Begin your sexual activity however you like, to the point where you're both physically and emotionally ready for the next steps. Then begin face-to-face intercourse. The penetrative partner is sending energy out through his penis. The penetrated partner takes the energy in through her vagina, pulls it up through her body, and sends it back out through her eyes into her partner, through his eyes. (She can also send it out through her mouth, kissing or blowing into her partner's mouth.) He takes the energy down from his eyes/mouth, through his body, and sends it back out through his penis.

What is happening here is that there is a circuit within a circuit. At a macro level, the sex itself is the polarity circuit—desirous connecting to desired, lover connecting to beloved. Often, even as desire and movement toward orgasm increase, there's a kind of grounding in the shift from "we want to have sex" to "we're having sex." The connection happens, the energy shifts into a higher gear, pleasure amps up, and a piece of it is grounded as some of those electrons reach their protons.

But here, at a micro level, there are circuits within circuits, polarities within polarities. We keep the circuit of polarity going throughout the sexual experience, continuing to cycle so that the magical energy is maintained rather than released. Eventually, yep, it's released, but by cycling it, a number of things happen: both partners are more satisfied, both partner's energies remain in balance with each other, and more magical power is available.

Love Polarity

It is possible to raise polar energy of desire and interconnection without sex. There are asexual romantic couples, for example, for whom this is more in tune with who they are.

The sexual cycle described above uses both emotion and sexuality. The "love only" version doesn't employ the genital connection but is basically the same.

Love is an exchange, an ongoing polarity of lover/beloved. We do things for one another. We give and we receive. That polarity is a normal part of our relationship. It can be consciously played upon for magical purposes, perhaps by enacting a simple exchange, such as handing a magical tool back and forth while maintaining eye contact.

The Third

There are myriad liminal states between male and female. When talking about morphology, there are quite a number of varieties of intersexuality. A 5-alpha-reductase deficiency, for example, is notable for being the condition belonging to Olympic gold medalist Caster Semenya, as well as the main character in the novel *Middlesex*. Other conditions include hypospadias, Klinefelter syndrome, and Turner syndrome.

For gender identity or expression, any nonbinary, genderqueer, or genderfluid identity stands as a third between male and female.

Three is also creation, so when talking about gendered bodies, we can obviously see fertility as a third, a new being emerging from heterosexual procreation.

Deities of Gender

In Kabbalah, the entire Pillar of **Mercy** is associated with male polarity, and the Pillar of **Severity** with female.

There aren't a whole lot of deities "of" women or men. To the extent that a particular deity is "a woman's goddess" or "a man's god," this deity is associated with other qualities. The mysteries of Mithra, for example, were secret and reserved for men only, but they were warrior mysteries, not gender mysteries. Gender-exclusive deities might be associated with coming of age, circumcision, menstruation, childbirth, or the men or women of a specific tribal heritage. None of that is gender *per se*.

Modern p-word practices have tended to perceive any and all goddesses as being "woman" and any and all gods as being "man." The Horned God of Wicca is often perceived as an exemplar of maleness, and the Mother Goddess of Wicca as femaleness. None of this necessarily provides insight into gender or gender polarity.

Another approach to finding deities of gender is to look at gender-shifting deities and stories. **Thor** dressed as a woman in a tale often seen as comedic, sometimes as humiliating, but it has been latched upon by queer people today. It's interesting that another thunder god—**Chango**—has a female form. In Santeria, the deities have syncretic forms of Catholic saints, and the very masculine Chango's form is Saint Barbara.

Loki transformed himself into a mare, mated with a stallion, and gave birth to Sleipnir, the eight-legged mount of Odin, thereby being a male god who experienced not merely being female, but actually giving birth and becoming a mother.

In Greek mythology, **Hermaphroditus,** the son of Hermes and Aphrodite, was turned into a two-gendered being when merged with the nymph **Salmacis. Tiresias,** the blind prophet, was turned into a woman for seven years before being turned back into a man.

In Hinduism, **Ardhanarishvara** is an aspect of Shiva, where half his body is male (Shiva) and half is female (Parvati). The name means "the god who is half a woman," and he is understood as male, but his body is divided vertically down the middle. (Images show the body clothed and do not show genitalia, although the female side has a distinct breast.)

This is just a sampling of deities with mixed-gender features, gender shifts, or cross-gender disguises. Any one of these stories requires an in-depth analysis to understand what it may be saying about gender, and naturally, cultural context matters.

Male and Female in Humanity

We may be in the first moment in human history where at least some people are not making assumptions about your very being based on gender. Historically, societies have ranged in how patriarchal they are (or are not), how accepting of gender differences they are, and how rigid they are about gender roles. But in every society, there have been assumptions, laws, and customs related to who you were, what you could do, what your inner nature was, and more, based on gender. There have been, in isolated cases, societies free of patriarchy, but not free of gender roles.

In many societies, up to and including today, men and women come together for sex and marriage, but actual relationship, as in warmth, friendship, and mutual understanding, exists primarily in same-sex relationships: family, friends, and colleagues. Women and men are seen as so fundamentally different from one another that true understanding cannot be expected. They are strangers who have love, sex, and children but not necessarily conversation.

It's ridiculous to try to enumerate the details of the ways in which gender and gender difference impacts human beings. It's simply outside the scope of this book to write a history of gender relations, or of patriarchy.

In a world where *Men Are from Mars, Women Are from Venus* is considered a "classic," it goes almost without saying that assumptions about gender, and indeed about gender polarity, permeate every part of our lives. There are many overt, spoken assumptions about gender, and many more unspoken, unexamined ones.

Setting aside sexism (which isn't easy), there's also a cultural assumption of gender essentialism. People are the way they are because of gender. They communicate the way they do, feel the way they do, want what they want, need what they need, because of gender. And it's easy to see that this gender essentialism—even when it's empowering, even when it lifts people up—is inherently not inclusive of nonbinary and nongender-normative people.

A lot of gender theorists tell us that gender is unimportant. Yet it continues to fascinate and compel us. We can't separate nature from nurture sufficiently to say what "is" male or female, yet it matters enough that trans people undergo major surgeries to affirm their genders. Gender dysphoria is a real condition, sort of proving that something within us finds gender so essential, so inescapable, that a mismatched body shape is agony.

Magical Tools of Gender

In some magical traditions, every tool is given a gender, but that's not particularly useful here.

In general, the tools most associated with maleness are the sword, ritual knife (athame), wand, and staff. They are all considered phallic. These tools thrust, penetrate, and divide, and are martial.

The tools most associated with femaleness are the cup, pentacle, paten, and cauldron. The cup and cauldron are yonic, having a vaginal shape. The cup is a container for beverages, while the paten and pentacle are plates, holding solid food. The cauldron is known in legend to hold either, as well as soups and stews, which are liminal nourishments composed of both solids and liquids. In Celtic legend, the cauldron is associated with bottomless nourishment, wisdom, and immortality. Doreen Valiente conflates these tools in the Charge of the Goddess:

Mine is the Cup of the Wine of Life, and the Cauldron of Cerridwen, which is the Holy Grail of Immortality.[154]

So the Great Mother who speaks the Charge says these are her tools, and her cup is conflated with her cauldron, and both are cognate with the Holy Grail.

Notice that the male tools can be seen as Severity, both because they're pretty harsh and because the blades (knife and sword) are used to *sever* things. Any magical tool can be called a "weapon," but these male tools are weapons in the mundane sense. By contrast, the female tools are tools of giving—they feed and replenish. It's interesting that this is exactly the opposite of the Kabbalistic correspondences of the genders. This creates internal polarities within each gender: a polarity of severity and mercy between tools and the Tree of Life.

It's also true that the male tools (as weapons) take life, while the female tools give it (as nourishment), creating a cycle of death and rebirth that is suggestive of the third created by this great polarity.

As mentioned in chapter 9, Tibetan Buddhism ascribes gender to the bell (female) and the dorje (male), its primary magical tools.

Gender Polarity in Ritual

It's almost unnecessary to describe a ritual that leverages male and female as polarity. If your occult training included anything about polarity, this is the polarity you were taught. This is the polarity found in a zillion books on magic, ritual, Wicca, ceremonial magic, and so on.

Fair warning: The following rituals are designed to be inclusive of nonbinary and gender-nonconforming people, but that doesn't mean they will work for everyone. Remember that there are other ways of working with polarity besides gender, and if gender isn't the right polarity for you, that's fine.

---

154. "The Charge of the Goddess," DoreenValiente.org.

Constructing Gender Polar Rituals by Role-Playing

One long-standing tradition in occultism is for men and women to have different roles. This can be enacting and embodying goddesses for women and gods for men (as in the Golden Dawn), women being the Priestess and men being the Priest (as in Thelema or Wicca), or other ritual roles. The gendered nature of these roles might have once been considered essential (and still are by many people), meaning that *of course* a woman must play the goddess and a man must play the god; but even understanding that they are *not* essential, the gender roles can be maintained as a way of layering gender polarity into the magic.

While embodying goddesses is considered the role of women in many traditions, and embodying gods is considered the role of men, there are other traditions where this is not at all true. African diaspora religions such as Santeria and Vodou, for example, have possession traditions in which anyone, of any gender, can be possessed by a spirit of any gender.

Many Western magical traditions, having learned from contact with other traditions, train priestesses and priests to embody deities of any gender. They may treat this as normative, or they may do it merely as a consciousness-expanding training exercise. My own experience of being a vessel for a male deity was the one and only time in my life when I experienced gender dysphoria. Not *during* the ritual, mind you, but in the days afterward, my sense-memory of my body being male was ever present, and decidedly uncomfortable. It was a valuable experience. In addition to the ritual value I gained, I, a cisgender woman very comfortable with my gender, also gained a tiny taste of what life can be like for my trans siblings.

Constructing Gender Polar Rituals by Contrast

As we've discussed, one idea of gender polarity that we find in occultism is that polarity energy is generated simply by men and women both being present in the same ritual. Rituals can be structured with that in mind. Polarity of contrast, remember, is when a drumbeat of back-and-forth is maintained between the poles. We did this in the force/form ritual in chapter 7, where everything was handed from Force to Form. We did a similar thing in the passive/active ritual in chapter 9, shifting between the two poles with each step of the ritual.

So we could add gender to either of those rituals if we chose, adding another shot of polarity energy by having the two partners be of different genders, however you define gender.

As I've mentioned, my early training in Wicca included rules about alternating gender constantly in ritual. To generate "polar (gender) energy," some groups even have taboos against people of the same sex touching at all, so that *all* touch is transmitted through a gender-polarity circuit. Through dozens of these trivial behaviors, polarity was being built up as an energy to add to the power of the rite. Many people I know have discarded such customs as unnecessary, and indeed, there's plenty of power available in rituals that don't leverage gender polarity. In some groups, the concept of gender polarity is inherently problematic. But if it works for all involved, it's a simple way to add polarity energy to your rituals.

"If it works for all involved," though, means two important things, the first being that everyone involved has a chance to discuss and weigh in on it. If anyone in your group is uncomfortable or feels excluded, you need to hear and honor that, and just because no one has spoken up yet doesn't mean they're comfortable. In a majority heteronormative group, your one nonbinary member might not be comfortable speaking up, so it's incumbent on the group leaders/organizers to pointedly open the conversation and assume nothing in advance. This includes conversations with newcomers before ever dropping anyone into a ritual situation that might be painful for them.

Second, we have discussed gender as defined by morphology, identity, and expression. When we ask ourselves *How did something as universal as gender become seen as oppressive?* the answer becomes obvious. It is when society—or someone other than the individual—imposes a gender on that individual. Almost always this is the assigned gender at birth.

As we've educated ourselves about gender, we've seen that even obvious physical indicators are not so obvious. Genitalia at birth don't always accurately predict what that body is going to look like after adolescence, and genitalia at birth, for intersex people, aren't always definitive—although gender will usually be assigned anyway (often to the detriment of the intersex person's wellbeing). Many of us *think* that gender, at least as defined by body shape, is something we can just *see*, but we've learned that is not true. Gender identity, as understood by the person whose gender we're discussing, is actually the most accurate and correct indicator of gender, not to mention the most respectful.

If you're using gender energies in your rituals, gender identity and/or expression are the *only* accurate and respectful ways of defining gender. If the gender identity of everyone in your group is the same as their assigned gender at birth, that's basically a coincidence.

Every magical group I've been involved with or encountered has some inherent respect for the trustworthiness and integrity of the magician built in, as expressed in phrases and principles such as perfect love and perfect trust, inner power, True Will, immanent deity, and the like. We can't do magic with one another if we don't believe in one another. I think it's obvious, then, that this includes believing one another's self-reported gender identity.

Gender-contrast rituals might not work for nonbinary people who aren't comfortable expressing gender at all, or who have been traumatized by being pushed to choose one gender or the other, but they might work powerfully for a diverse set of heteronormative, gender-nonconforming, and queer people who are all able to resonate with gender energies in a polar way.

Ritual of Blessing

This simple ritual blesses a group by offering them food. Here, Priestess and Priest each carry a tool that matches their gender. Polarity/contrast is generated by the genders (identity, expression, or role, as they choose) separating and meeting. Priestess and Priest each have a separate job, and the Priestess interacts only with male-identified people (called "men" here), while the Priest interacts with only female-identified people (called "women").

YOU'LL NEED

- A ritual knife and a plate (paten) of food prepared for the occasion (Perhaps it has been blessed or charged as part of the ritual.)

Priest and Priestess walk around the circle together. They start with her holding the paten and him holding the knife. They go to the first man.

Priestess: (Holding out paten) *I offer you food of blessing.*

Man: (Takes a cake / cookie / whatever from the paten)

Priestess: (Hands paten to Priest and takes knife from him; points knife at Man, drawing a pentagram over him) *I charge and consecrate you to take in and be empowered by this food of blessing.*

Man: *I accept this blessing.* (They can kiss or touch.)

Priestess and Priest now go to the first woman in the circle.

Priest: (Holding out paten, which he still has from the previous blessing) *I offer you food of blessing.*

Woman: (Takes a cake / cookie / whatever from the paten)

Priest: (Hands paten to Priestess and takes knife from her; points knife at Woman, drawing a pentagram over her) *I charge and consecrate you to take in and be empowered by this food of blessing.*

Woman: *I accept this blessing.* (They can kiss or touch.)

Repeat for each person in the circle, with the Priestess serving and consecrating all men and the Priest serving and consecrating all women.

Constructing Gender Polar Rituals by Sublimation

In contrast, the poles interact and interact and interact. In sublimation, they are held apart, a long, drawn-out tease, until they finally come together in a magical *wham,* a moment of ecstasy through which the built-up power flows.

For example, this is part of a traditional wedding, where the betrothed are separated prior to the wedding for some period of time, only seeing each other again when they are about to marry. The love/lust energy, and perhaps the identity and/or expression energy, is held apart, only to be brought together at the culmination of the ceremony, creating a crashing wave of power entering the couple and the marriage.

In an occult ceremony, this can be emphasized by holding tools and other symbols apart as well. A male-identified partner only touches "male" tools, and a female-identified partner only touches "female" tools.

Marriage Vow Blessing Ritual

Here, the "groom" is the male-identified partner and the "bride" is the female-identified partner. You can do this with two brides, two grooms, or any designation of about-to-be-wed that is comfortable for you. If you are working with love/lust energy and not identifying either partner as gendered, choose the tools however you prefer.

YOU'LL NEED

- The wedding rings and a wand that they fit over

The bride and groom have not touched each other at all prior to the wedding for a period of time that they have decided is appropriate and have not yet touched during the wedding ceremony.

Officiant: *It is now time to exchange rings.*

Bride: (Holds up rings) *I bring my blessing to these rings and prepare to join with my beloved.*

Groom: (Holds up wand) *I bring my blessing to these rings and prepare to join with my beloved.*

(**Bride** slips rings over wand, as if the wand were a finger.)

(**Groom** places his hands over the bride's hands, so that both are holding the rings over the wands, sending their joined energy into the rings.)

Officiant: *[Groom], repeat after me: [Insert marriage vows here.]*

Groom: (Repeats marriage vows)

Officiant: *[Bride], repeat after me: [Insert marriage vows here.]*

Bride: (Repeats marriage vows)

The wedding proceeds from this point.

Constructing Gender-Polar Rituals of Liminality

With liminality, energy is seen as flowing from one pole to the other on a journey that acquires energy during the in-between leg of that journey. In other words, power is found not just in the movement from pole A to pole B, but in the stops along the way. The liminal space transforms one pole into the other— liminality holds the energy of becoming, of the shift from one state to another. We saw this with night and day, but most occultists aren't used to constructing gender ritual this way.

Using liminality energy is a way of exploring gender energy that is inclusive of people who aren't comfortable expressing any binary energy, even in the temporary context of "for tonight's ritual." (Remember, though, that some nonbinary people don't perceive their gender as being on a pole at all. Some nonbinary people are not "between" male and female; they're both/and, or neither/nor, or in a blended state that doesn't map well to the analogy of a pole.)

I see two ways of constructing liminal gender rituals. One is using the idea of a battery intercepting energy. As discussed earlier, with a battery-operated toothbrush, the battery intercepts the electrons as they move toward the protons. So you can construct a gender ritual where a nonbinary participant's role is to intercept energy being sent from male to female or from female to male. In a spell, for example, the binary-gendered people would raise the energy and the nonbinary people would collect that energy and send it to the target.

A second method (the one in the following sample ritual) is to set aside the electron/proton thing entirely and use the journey as a source of power, emphasizing the magic of liminality itself. In chapter 11 we talked about the power of the crossroads; nonbinary gender is such a crossroads. You could build a ritual including only nonbinary people, leaning into gender as a source of liminal power, or you could build a ritual inclusive of binary and nonbinary gender by continually moving from male to nonbinary to female to nonbinary to male, and so on. Since it's more of a circle than a line, I don't think a single cycle of binary to nonbinary to binary makes sense without the return.

Consecration Ritual

Use this simple ritual to consecrate an object using liminal gender energies. Ideally this is an object without a specific gender assignment. To consecrate a phallic or yonic tool, liminal energy isn't necessarily the best match. On the other hand, a piece of jewelry, a deity, or many other altar pieces or magical objects could be consecrated this way.

This ritual assumes three people: a man or male-identified person, a woman or female-identified person, and a person identifying as nonbinary or liminal. One of these people is the owner of the object being consecrated.

Owner: *We do now consecrate this [object] by our power and our will. Be it blessed by the energies we raise here that it may be used for [purpose].*

Woman: *[Object], be blessed and empowered by the energy I bring.* (Woman holds object close to her heart, visualizing gender/polar energy entering the object. When ready, she hands the object to the nonbinary participant.)

Nonbinary Person: *[Object], be blessed and empowered by the energy I bring.* (Nonbinary Person holds object close to their heart, visualizing liminal energy entering the object. When ready, they hand the object to the man.)

Man: *[Object], be blessed and empowered by the energy I bring.* (Man holds object close to his heart, visualizing gender/polar energy entering the object. When ready, he hands the object to the nonbinary participant.)

Nonbinary Person: *[Object], be blessed and empowered by the energy we all bring.* (Nonbinary Person visualizes the object containing a moving flow of all energies already sent. When ready, they hand the object to the woman.)

Woman: *[Object], you are blessed by a circle of energy.* (Woman visualizes her energy as sealing the circle.)

All: (Signaled by a nod from the woman) *So be it!*

Journal/Discussion Prompts

- Are you comfortable with using gender polarity in ritual? Why or why not?
- Do these feelings change depending on whether gender polarity is based on body, identity, or expression?
- What does it feel like to work with gender polarity by contrast?
- What does it feel like to work with gender polarity by sublimation?
- What does it feel like to work with gender liminality?

SECTION THREE
WHAT'S NEXT?

Section Three

Toward a Nonbinary Future

When I began this book, my outline ended at the end of section 2, but as I came closer to finishing, I realized I had left an unanswered question: *Now what?*

What can you do with the new knowledge of polarity that this book has presented? You walk away, I hope, better informed about the misconceptions and realities of polarity energy, as it relates to gender and otherwise. In fact, you may have learned a bit about gender as well.

Perhaps you're wondering about incorporating polarity into magic and spellwork in a practical way. Perhaps you're part of a polarity-based magical system of some kind, and you are left with a quandary about how to incorporate your new knowledge into that system. Or perhaps you're part of a system that doesn't use polarity at all, and you're wondering if you can introduce some of these energies.

Our concluding pages will address all of these questions.

Chapter Thirteen

Polarity Magic

What does it mean to do polarity magic? We can break this down broadly into two areas: doing magic in which the primary source of energy is polarity (polarity magic) and doing magic in which polarity energy is added to whatever else you're doing (magic that *includes* polarity). We can also determine what kind of polar energy we're using.

The Meaning of Polar Energies

Traditional occultism tends to equate all polar energies with all other polar energies. Everything is yin and yang, female and male, passive and active, form and force. Everything exists on the Pillar of Severity or the Pillar of Mercy.

Correspondences like this can add profound insight. It's also true, though, that treating each polarity as a unique energy adds nuance. Your individual magical working might benefit more from a force/form energy, or from a passive/active energy, or from one of the many other energies we've discussed. Look at the polarities in the chart in appendix B. Does one of these jump out at you as deeply connected to the work? If so, *use* that connection.

For example, for theurgic work to deepen your connection to your gods or angels, you might build *self and other* into your ritual—specifically, *humanity and divinity* (see "Simple Altar Work with Polarity" later in this chapter for an example). A major turning point in your life might be a good time to leverage the polarity of *choice and fate.*

For weather magic, you might add the polarity of *moon and sun* or *earth and sky* to your ritual. You could do this, for example, by emphasizing the distance between earth and sky, symbolically bringing the two together using tools, words, chants, or simple actions, and using the spell itself as the interceptor of that energy, as it traverses the distance between you on earth and the weather patterns in the sky.

Polar Magic

In *Magical Power for Beginners,* I define spells as follows:

> A spell is a series of steps taken to achieve a magical goal. Those steps, in their most basic form, are *(1) focus your intention, (2) create your connection, (3) raise power, (4) send power,* and *(5) finish the spell.*[155]

Let's start with the understanding that polarity's primary impact will be on step 3—polarity is a form of energy and therefore a form of raising power.

Magic works best with a consistent through line. In addition, when you perform a spell in a way that is consistent with the goal of the spell, it tends to increase the effectiveness of the magic. What does this mean? Consistency from beginning to end means that polarity won't be confined to a box that is defined by raising power, but rather that it will be present throughout the entire experience. Consistency with the goal means that polar energy might be particularly meaningful in spells for couples, or for relationships, or to create balance, or to end stagnation (which is kind of like *unbalancing*), or for attraction, or for any other purpose consistent with polar energies.

Here are some examples of magical goals that might be especially empowered by polarity:

- Healing (Virtually all healing restores the body's balance.)

---

155. Lipp, *Magical Power for Beginners,* 18–19.

- Theurgy generally (The *self and other* polarity can be leveraged whenever we are connecting to a spiritual being.)
- Relationships (healing an existing relationship or attracting new relationships, whether romance, friendship, or any other)
- Job magic (based on attraction between the job and the job seeker)
- Creating order, structure, or "getting it together" (shifting from *Dionysian* to *Apollonian*)
- Creativity or new projects (*Force and form* join to bring forth creation.)

You can also use polar energies for any blessing, assuming the energies are sacred and bring blessedness.

Raising the Polarity Energy

The rituals in section 2 of this book raise polarity energy as part of other rituals, as a means of exploring those energies, or as an end unto themselves. Any of these examples, and any other creative use of polarity, can be used in magic.

Remember electrons and protons. A polar circuit is an electron seeking a proton, generating energy as it moves toward the proton and then neutralizing the energy when they meet. The most straightforward way to leverage polar energy in magic is to place that which is to be energized between the poles, so that it intercepts the energy before it is neutralized.

You can raise the power through contrast: come together and quickly separate, come together and quickly separate, over and over until the final connection. Or you can raise power through sublimation, keeping the poles apart for as long as possible until completion.

Example: Consecrating a Talisman with Polarity

In this example, a couple is consecrating a talisman to wear for bringing general or specific blessings. I'll give two sets of polarity steps: one for gender polarity, assuming some sort of polarity between the two (they are a heterosexual couple or have expressive polarity such as butch/femme), and the other for passive/active polarity.

(1) Focus Your Intention

Gender polarity: Partner A states the intention aloud and hands the talisman to Partner B with a kiss. Partner A states the intention aloud and places it on the altar.

Passive/active: Passive opens their hands to receive the talisman. Active states the intention aloud and places the talisman in Passive's hands. Active then takes the talisman from Passive and places it on the altar.

(2) Create Your Connection

This step creates a sympathetic or imitative connection to the target of the magic. For example, in a healing, you might make a connection to a distant subject through a photograph. Since the target is the talisman already present on the altar, extra steps aren't needed.

(3) Raise Power and (4) Send Power

Gender polarity: Power could be raised and then sent through sex magic. (See the section on sex magic later in this chapter for examples.)

Another option (among many!) is to pass the object back and forth with a kiss or other touch while chanting or intoning. Use a single word or phrase to sum up the meaning of the talisman, such as "Blessings" (kiss), "blessings" (kiss), "blessings" (kiss), back and forth, back and forth, allowing the power to gradually build, culminating at peak in sending the power while embracing tightly, both holding the talisman.

Passive/active: With the talisman on the altar between them, the partners face each other. Active's role is to send energy into Passive. Passive's role is to receive the energy. The talisman, between them, intercepts the energy as it moves back and forth.

Active says "I give," followed by Passive saying "I receive." This goes back and forth, focusing on the energy, "I give"/"I receive"/"I give"/"I receive." This builds gradually, going faster and faster. At the point where it's going so fast that the partners are speaking simultaneously, send all the power into the talisman.

An alternate version is to continuously switch the roles of passive and active back and forth between the two people. Some people will find this easier, while some will find it confusing.

Person A (now active): *I give.*

Person B (now passive): *I receive.*

Person B (now active): *I give.*

Person A (now passive): *I receive.*

This continues as before, back and forth, faster and faster, with power being sent when the energy is at peak and speaking is simultaneous.

(5) Finish the Spell

Declare success ("so mote it be" or "it is done" or the like). Always seal spells by *using* the object of the spell. In this case, the talisman should be put on. If it's for someone else, it should immediately be placed in its packaging for delivery to the owner. Then complete the polarity circuit by embracing (for gender) or formally declaring an end to the passive/active polarity. If one partner has been active and one passive the entire time, briefly reverse the polarity (have the passive partner give something to the active partner) so that the cycle is ended.

Example: Adding Polarity to the Work of Your Altar

In chapter 8 we mentioned divinity and humanity as a polarity akin to self and other. We recognize the polar tension in "I am not you; we are apart" when we seek to worship or commune with a deity or other spiritual being.

We do this even when we also recognize that we *are* alike, we *are* the same. If you are a believer in immanent deity—that the gods are within you—you are still doing some sort of work to commune with deity. Whether you perceive deity as wholly outside of you, wholly within you, or some combination, you are still not experiencing yourself *as* deity on a day-to-day basis. For you, the work might be more like creating an inner connection rather than connecting to an other, but there remains a distance to traverse.

There are as many different ways that occultists work with their personal altars as there are occultists—probably more. Here I will offer a very simple pair of examples from my own practice at an altar: first a basic altar ritual without polarity, and then the same ritual with a polarity component added.

Simple Altar Work (without Polarity)

1. Prepare the altar by cleaning and tidying it. Bring whatever offerings are needed (incense, fresh water, flowers, etc.).

2. Ground and center, becoming fully present.

3. Meditate on the deity or being you are connecting to.

4. State out loud a greeting and your intention. For example: *Jai Ganesha, hail to thee, remover of obstacles. I bring myself before thee for blessings and to honor thee.*

5. Optionally, use any tools you choose while greeting your deity (such as ringing a bell or pointing a wand).

6. Make offerings as appropriate, perhaps describing them out loud and asking that they be accepted: *I bring incense, I bring clear spring water, I bring marigolds. Accept these offerings, O Lord.*

7. Meditate on the experience of your offering being accepted.

8. Close with a word of thanks and perhaps another use of a tool.

Simple Altar Work with Polarity

Additional polarity steps are in **bold**.

1. Prepare the altar by cleaning and tidying it. Bring whatever offerings are needed (incense, fresh water, flowers, etc.). **Arrange the altar so that the image/idol of the deity is at the back and offerings are between you and the image/idol. Be sure the altar also includes an offering bowl, as idol/offering bowl are a pair of tools denoting this polarity.**

2. Ground and center, becoming fully present.

3. Meditate on the deity or being you are connecting to. **Visualize the polarity between divinity and humanity. Feel the longing in yourself to move toward divinity. Concentrate on the image of the deity while sending a rush of energy along that pole.**

4. State out loud a greeting and your intention. **Include a statement of polarity.** For example: *Jai Ganesha, hail to thee, remover of obstacles.* **Mortal to immortal. Human to divine. Incarnate to transcendent.** *I bring myself before thee for blessings and to honor thee.*

5. Optionally, use any tools you choose while greeting your deity (such as ringing a bell or pointing a wand).

6. Make offerings as appropriate, perhaps describing them out loud and asking that they be accepted. **As you make offerings, note the connection of the tools (bowl and idol) to this polarity. The offering bowl is the mediating space between human and divinity. With your gestures, allow the offering to demonstrate the movement from human to divine.** *I bring incense, I bring clear spring water, I bring marigolds.* **From me to thee, from human to God, I send offerings.** *Accept these offerings, O Lord.*

7. Meditate on the experience of your offering being accepted **and on polarity being grounded in the connection between human and divine.**

8. Close with a word of thanks and perhaps another use of a tool.

Sex Magic

There are many techniques of sex magic, including ones that intentionally use polarity and ones that do not. As author Lee Harrington says:

The fundamental concept in sex magic is that libido and sexual energy have the power to create altered states of consciousness and facilitate theurgical, magical, and religious work....Some form of sex magic has been prevalent in every single culture across the globe.[156]

Although polarity energy is always present in sex between two people, its energy can be *consciously* added to sex magic by creating focus on the sexual polarity circuit as described in chapter 12, as well as by structuring the sex magic ritual in a way that optimizes the circuit—placing that which is to be empowered between the poles as they move toward each other, and allowing the grounding to happen only afterward.

Not Necessarily Polar

Sex magic doesn't have to be polar. Notice that the above quote doesn't even mention polarity. Polarity raises power and is associated with sex, but other things that raise power and are associated with sex include pleasure, transcendence, and movement. As I mentioned in chapter 3, sex as energy raising isn't necessarily any different from drumming and dancing. But sexual energy tends to lend itself easily to polarity work because the contrast of energies coming together has an inherently polar quality.

A typical act of sex magic is something like: focusing on a magical goal during a sexual act, maintaining that focus as sexual intensity climbs, and, in the moment before orgasm, releasing that energy toward the goal, with the orgasm itself acting as a final thrust, pushing the energy, already in flight, the rest of the way. There are many, many variations on this, including separating the sexual energy from the concentration in different ways (which is handy because it's hard to concentrate during sex), avoiding orgasm entirely in order to maintain the power of the sexual crescendo, using specified positions, and so on. There's group sex magic and solitary sex magic as well as the more traditional couple sex magic.

Adding Polarity to Sex Magic

In *Magical Power for Beginners*, I describe one way of separating sexual energy from concentration:

---

156. Harrington, *Sacred Kink*, 133.

Partner A maintains a clear visualization of the target while bringing Partner B to orgasm. B's entire job is to raise as much sex energy as possible and, at the moment of orgasm, send it all to A.[157]

Partner A then takes B's sexual energy and sends it to the target of the spell. Partner A's job is to concentrate, visualize, and form the magic, while Partner B's job is energy raising alone. The couple can complete their sexual experience after the magic—that is, Partner B can subsequently bring Partner A to orgasm, outside the context of the spell, if they choose.

Now, we can view this as not polar at all—it's just a handy structure for energy raising. But knowing what we know about polarity, we can see that in this scenario, Partner B is force, creating energy without any effort at shaping it, while Partner A is form, giving shape and purpose to that energy. In my former marriage, we found this worked best with me as Partner B and my husband as Partner A. Men who are good partners to women often train themselves to delay their orgasm and be other-directed in order to make sure their partners get off. That experience lends itself perfectly to this kind of magic. It's funny to me that my traditional heterosexual sex magic ended up with female=force and male=form. I think the ancient Kabbalistic sages were missing something!

In sex, certain qualities are present that can be understood as polar, for example, the *force* of orgasmic energy, which we see can be leveraged using force and form. Orgasmic energy tends to feel chaotic and can be contrasted with order. The same ritual separation described above can be interpreted as Partner A representing order (structuring the ritual and imposing a visualization on it), while Partner B is chaos (formless energy is chaotic). Fucked and fucker, desired and desire, and gender (sometimes) are also polar energies that are readily accessible during sex magic.

Example: Creating Attraction with Sex Magic

In this example, the couple will use the force/form polarity. I won't gender the couple, and will use they/them pronouns.

---

157. Lipp, *Magical Power for Beginners*, 173.

Attraction magic is a natural fit for sex magic. Examples of attraction magical purposes include:

- Attracting a new partner, including adding a partner to a polyamorous relationship
- Attracting a person for a specific group, such as a new musician for your band or a new witch for your coven
- Attracting buyers for your home or tenants for your rental property
- Finding a new home for yourselves

Attraction is frequently visualized as a beam that is brightly visible to the intended target but invisible to others. I like to use a lighthouse. My teacher liked a ribbon or rope that the intended target would grab on to, with the magical energy then pulling the target home.

Sex magic is often used to empower an item—a talisman, amulet, or symbol of the magical intention. The item is created prior to the sex magic, either in a separate magical ritual or with intention but without ritual. In the example of consecrating a talisman earlier in this chapter, there was, similarly, a preliminary step of creating the talisman.

Perhaps you are a polyamorous couple who wishes to expand your relationship; you ideally envision a triad. You could create a token representing the unknown third person. Sitting together, generating loving focus with eye contact, you place a consecrated paper and pen between you. Draw a big heart or other symbol that appeals to you on the paper. Now imagine out loud who the ideal partner might be, suggesting words and phrases like *playful, smart, adventurous,* or *happiness.* Once you've settled on one or two words at most, write the word or phrase in the center of the paper, inside the heart/symbol. Then each of you sign your name on either side of the phrase, so that you've placed all three of you, connected, in the heart. Fold up the paper so that all the names and words touch each other inside the heart, tie it with a ribbon, and you have your magical attraction token.

(1) Focus Your Intention

Form prepares the space, since making the bed, setting out the sex toys and lube, and other physical actions inherently give shape and use form energy. Force can focus on generating sexual energy in whatever way is comfortable for you as a couple, including setting up any sexy atmosphere (music, candles, or whatever you like).

Form states the intention out loud, simply, in an affirmative way, such as "The partner we desire comes to us."

(2) CREATE YOUR CONNECTION

Holding up the token, Form names it: "This is the partner who will come." Then Form takes the token and places it between themselves and their partner—in their hands or between their bodies, however they choose. During sex, Form can hold the token, or they both can hold it together, or it can be used as part of the sex, gently running it over one another's bodies, joining Force, Form, and the intermediary token in a single act.

(3) RAISE POWER

Force now releases any thought of magical intent and just focuses on their body, their libido, and their pleasure. Nothing else is present for them.

Form holds the intention in mind while focusing most of their attention on bringing sexual pleasure to Force. As Force comes closer to orgasm, Form amplifies and shapes that energy, mentally taking the libidinous power and moving it toward the intention.

(4) SEND POWER

As Force begins to orgasm, Form concentrates on sending the power to attracting the partner—creating the light beam or whatever visualization you've decided on. Keep the visualization going throughout the peak. As orgasm ends, Form embraces Force tightly, sending the last of the energy and grounding it.

(5) FINISH THE SPELL

Declare success and place the token someplace previously agreed upon. (If it's under the doormat, throw on a robe first!) Force can now continue the sex, giving Form a chance to enjoy orgasm, or perhaps you both want to enjoy more sex peaks, or you can just cuddle, as you choose.

Masturbation

Sex magic can leverage polar energy even when practiced alone, using masturbation, by visualizing the circuit as an internal physical and psychic experience. We know that we contain all poles within ourselves. It's much easier to express poles in partnership, but it's not a requirement.

How would this be done? You'd start with a clear visualization. For example, think about the polarity of matter and energy. Feel the sexual desire building up within you as energy, irresistible and shapeless. Now find matter within you, the shape and structure that you will bring to that energy. As you use your hands, your vibrator, etc., visualize the matter, the reality, emerging from your intention. Imagine the energy of desire moving toward the matter of the physical act of masturbation. Then your magical intention can be added to the process, the activity that moves your energy into matter, into the state of completion and orgasm.

Perhaps you could even state your intention out loud as you begin, using either an "I will" or an "I am" statement (*I am matter, I am energy, energy seeking toward matter, matter fulfilling energy*) or using the voice of a pole speaking to the other pole (*I feel you, desirous energy, and I come to bring you shape and fulfillment*). You can make it formal or sexy or playful or whatever you like. There's no audience but you, so feel free to experiment!

Another idea is a variation on the passive/active solitary ritual in chapter 9 ("A Solitary Ritual of Active/Passive"). One thing that is often true about masturbation is that it's an escape and release from ordinary, non-sexual, non-playful life. You're turning off the workday, public part of your brain and/or body and focusing on the personal, sexual, and private. So, as in the chapter 9 ritual, an active part of you is shifting to passive and a silent part is awakening. Visualizing this shift can help you access internal polarity.

Adding Polar Energy to Magic

Any magic or ritual you already do can have polar energies added to it. Often, it already has polar energies and it's simply a matter of teasing them out and making them conscious. Figure out what polarity you're using and how your ritual is already constructed, and find natural spots for including polarity. Here are some ideas:

- *For a group ritual to include gender polarity:* Have male-identified and female-identified people stand alternately, and hand tools and objects only male-to-female or female-to-male. (As mentioned, this is a tradition in some forms of Wicca.)

- *For a group or partnered ritual to include the force/form polarity:* Have the Force partner empower each tool and object before handing it to the Form partner to use. Have all creative steps first charged by the Force partner and then performed by the Form partner.

- *For a solitary ritual:* Have tools of the polarity being used on your altar, and alternate using each, moving the energy back and forth while visualizing that energetic movement. (Since each chapter in section 2 references tools of that polarity, you can easily find tools for any polarity being worked.)

- *For a solitary ritual:* Have a diagram of the Tree of Life on your altar. Move tools or magical objects from one sphere to another, for example, from Chokmah to Binah to generate force/form energy. (See Appendix A: Polarity on the Tree of Life.)

- *For a solitary ritual:* Pause between steps of your ritual that could be represented by one pole or another to focus on that energy. For example, for each active step taken in a ritual, immediately stop and wait afterward, seeing the active energy flow into that passive moment and then becoming active again. This works well for passive/active, force/form, night/day, etc.

- *In a group ritual:* Have everyone identified with one pole on one side of the space and everyone identified with the other pole on the other side. Perform every step twice—first by one pole, then the other. At the peak of the ritual, have everyone come together.

Chapter Fourteen

Occult Groups

How do you bring a new understanding of polarity to a group you are currently a part of or groups you may join in the future? If you are a solitary occultist, this isn't an issue, as you can work on inner polarity to the extent that you're comfortable with. If you're partnered, it's a matter of the two of you figuring out exactly the kind of magical partnership that works for you. But in a group, there are other dynamics at play, including an established tradition, rules that may currently govern the group, or simply the ideas and attitudes of other group members.

Polarity-Based Systems

If you're a part of a tradition or magical system or lodge or what have you based in polarity, you may be looking at that system differently right now. It is almost certain that your tradition equates polarity with gender and may define it as "gender polarity." We've learned in these pages that polarity isn't necessarily tied to gender, but it's been characterized and explained that way for over a hundred years.

First of all, there is no need for queer and nonbinary people to walk away from polarity systems. In fact, the initial inspiration for this book came from just that situation. I'm a queer person who has no desire to leave my polarity-based tradition, and I wanted to explore that. It ended up being a deeper and more interesting exploration than I ever could have imagined.

There are definitely people who will tell you that you don't belong in a polarity system if you're queer or nonbinary. But you are the only person who gets to decide where you belong in this world. If you feel at home in your tradition, I honor that feeling. If you *do* feel at home, you may still be wondering now how to approach ideas about polarity that may be old-fashioned or incorrect.

First, there's absolutely no need to accept or tolerate ideas about gender that are scientifically incorrect. Bigots love to tell you that "science" and "biology" inform their ideas about gender, but it's science they learned in the third grade—and they know it. If they're smart enough to form long-winded screeds on the internet, they're smart enough to read the kind of scientific information, presented for the layperson, that I read in order to write the science section in chapter 1. They choose not to, because they choose to cling to their bigotry. While I don't think anyone has to leave their tradition if it works for them, I also don't think any of us should be doing ritual or magic with people who don't accept who we are.

If there are people in your tradition or system who are telling you that gender is defined solely by genitalia, they're wrong. And it is very unlikely they speak for the whole of their tradition. I know a Gardnerian coven that does not accept trans people as their authentic gender. And I know of a few other covens, within thirty miles of that one, that do. The transphobic coven probably thinks the other covens are doing it wrong, but they're all authentically Gardnerian.

That said, not everyone is cut out to be a social justice warrior or has an interest in fighting the system. You may be part of a system with prescribed gender roles, and you may have no interest in changing that. That's okay—assuming that "gender" means *gender* and not *genitalia*, and assuming it's not about bigotry, that is.

Gender can be a powerful way of expressing polarity, as we've explored. It can also be a label or framework for other polarities. Many of the "gender" polarities in Wicca, for example, have underpinnings of force and form. "Male" is a framework by which to express force, and "female" is the expression of form. The Golden Dawn defines *female* as the passive polarity and *male* as the active. You may choose to work with "gender polarity" as defined by your tradition while seeing the true polarity energies as other than gendered. You might do this simply because you like your tradition as it is and don't want to change it; you just want to understand it differently. You may be perfectly comfortable hearing the word *female* and redefining it as "passive" in your head. You may also be comfortable having conversations about that redefinition with the other members of your group.

Or you may take a more direct approach and remove gender from the equation, handing out roles based on force and form (or whatever the polarity is) without regard to the genders of the participants. You might change the language of your rituals where gendered terms are used by exploring what the underpinning polarity is and using that instead. You may find rich explorations of your tradition in the act of determining exactly what the polarity being expressed in any given ritual act actually is. I hope the explorations of many individual polarities in this book will help you do exactly that, if you choose to do so.

For example, your tradition may have a ritual in which "priestess" is doing X and "priest" is doing Y. Ask yourself: Exactly what is happening here? What is the priestess doing that the priest cannot do? What energies is the priestess using here, and how are the priest's energies functioning in contrast to that? Look for clues in the language of the ritual and its intended results. In my experience, these rituals are almost always force/form or passive/active in their intention (in large part because they descend from the Golden Dawn, where these were the major polarities in use). If you're not sure what the polar energy of a particular ritual is, perform it as written and then perform it again gender-swapped. Doing this will allow you to experience what flows and what doesn't when the swap occurs, and what the energy is like. Especially if you've done this ritual a lot, the people who normally occupy each role might not be aware of the energies as polar—they just *are*. Swapping gives a powerful new perspective. It allows the priestess and priest, accustomed to their prior roles, to experience energies internally that they previously only experienced indirectly. In my experience, I've learned more about the role I traditionally play, as well as the role I do not traditionally play, when I experiment this way. Some of these experiments become permanent changes and some do not, but the perspective is always valuable.

I'm not interested in tearing down my tradition or anyone else's. I like the idea of tradition, and I like doing things "because that's how they've always been done." There isn't a deep or important reason why turkey is more delicious than roast beef on Thanksgiving; it's eaten because it's a tradition and for no other reason. Even if you want to dismantle some of the traditions in your group that you find harmful, I don't encourage you to go after your system as a whole.

And, finally, you may choose to walk away. Again, if that's the right choice for you, I honor it.

Nonpolarity Systems

If the system or tradition you're a part of doesn't use polarity at all, you're in luck. The sky's the limit.

If you approach the members of your group with the idea of exploring polarity energies, they're likely to think you've suddenly become gender essentialist. Be prepared to explain what you mean! This book provides rituals and exercises for exploring polarity, and most groups enjoy having new exercises to experiment with.

Indeed, I don't recommend starting with the gender experiments, which come with a lot of cultural baggage. Perhaps you can start with self and other—the Self/Other Circle rite in chapter 8 is great for building group solidarity energy while exploring polarity. That might be just what you need to establish that these rituals are a safe space for exploration, and you can branch out from there.

Many of these rituals, and the discussion prompts that follow, can easily lead to new rituals, new experiments, and new discussions. You and your group might find yourself on an enthusiastic polarity journey!

In Conclusion

Long ago, I was taught that polarity was a fundamental energy of the universe. It was inherent in all magic and all ritual because of this fundamental nature. It was typified by, and expressed via, gender.

I was as queer when I was initiated in 1982 as I am today, but I was also much more accepting of gender normativity and gender essentialism. I didn't see a problem with aligning gender roles with polarity work, and I wasn't alone. The use of terms like *nonbinary, gender normative,* and *gender essentialist* outside of academic or politically focused circles is fairly new. Lots of people who identified as feminist and/or LGBT (the Q came later) were comfortable with standard definitions of gender, both inside and outside of their occult lives. This persisted throughout almost all of the twentieth century. The passionate belief in a mythic "ancient matriarchy," prevalent in Wicca, Paganism, and goddess spirituality in the 1970s and 1980s, was gender essentialist at its core—women were a particular way, and the fact that this particular way was seen as elevated didn't erase that.

Gradually, questions and concerns about "gender polarity" began to capture my attention. Still queer, still happily practicing a polarity system, I heard those questions as a knock-knock-knock on my door that persisted and grew louder. When things bother me, I explore them through thinking, experimentation, and writing. So perhaps this book was inevitable.

In these pages we've explored the origins of polarity and identified key moments in its development as an occult concept. We've looked deeply at the relationship between polarity and gender, both historically and in magical practice. We've found numerous expressions of polarity energy and explored them in theoretical and practical ways.

We've discovered that, indeed, polarity *is* a fundamental and universal energy, and it's almost always present if we look for it. There are other universal energies to be sure, and magic doesn't live or die by whether or not we leverage polarity. But it's there, not just to be used in magic and ritual but also to deepen our understanding of ourselves, our relationships to others, and our connection to deity. I suppose this is true of any universal energy—as we study it, we study ourselves. "As the universe, so the soul."

Polarity *can* be expressed by gender in ritual, as well as in many other ways. It has been used to oppress, but it can also celebrate, explore, and enrich.

In these final pages, we've briefly explored how polarity energy and polarity magic can be a part of your life. Polarity can be incorporated into spells, worship, meditation, and ritual of all kinds. It can enhance your existing occult practice or give you new paths to walk.

The rest is up to you.

Appendix A

Polarity on the Tree of Life

The idea to correspond each polarity to sephirot on the Tree of Life came to me late in the process of writing this book. Force and form are traditional descriptors for Chokmah and Binah, so once I decided to include them, I thought it would be interesting to go on and find correspondences for all the others.

I came to each correspondence through meditation and discussion, as a part of writing each chapter. Only when I got to the end did I realize it all mapped out perfectly, with no repeated sephirot and none left out. In the following illustration, it looks as if I had a plan from the beginning, but I did not. Six pairs, one of which (male and female) is traditionally and anciently associated with the pillars rather than individual sephirot, leaving five pairs for ten spheres, and it all comes out right.

The serendipity of this arrangement validates, for me, that I've chosen six polarities that are in some way essential, and it opens up the Kabbalah as a means of further exploration. This is exciting because the Kabbalah is structured around polarity, and extremely gendered, but also can be read as queer and empowering of nonbinary and blended-binary states.[158] I offer the following illustration for meditation, exploration, and enjoyment.

---

158. After I finished the first draft of this book, I was given an advance copy of *Queer Qabala* by Enfys Book, which I've added to the reference section as an excellent resource if this subject interests you.

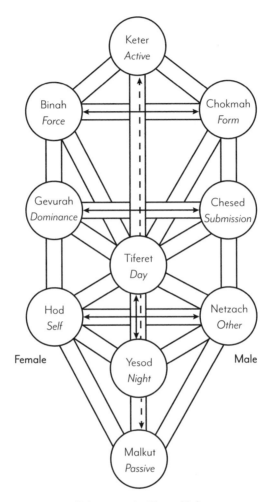

Polarity on the Tree of Life

Appendix B

Polarities Charts

Polarities of Force and Form

Force	Form
Energy	Matter
Spirit	Matter
Seed	Vessel
Plow	Field
Time	Space
Choice	Fate
History	Geography
Add your own:	

Polarities of Self and Other

Self	Other
Humanity	Divinity
Lover	Beloved
Immanence	Transcendence
Contraction	Expansion
Conjoin	Dissolve
Subject	Object
Planet	Satellite
Add your own:	

Polarities of Passive and Active

Passive	Active
Stasis	Movement
Fucked	Fucker
Socket	Plug
Receptive	Projective
Being	Becoming
Add your own:	

Polarities of Dominance and Submission

Dominance	Submission
Top	Bottom
Control	Surrender
Apollonian	Dionysian
Order	Chaos
Center	Circumference

Add your own:

Polarities of Night and Day

Night	Day
Moon	Sun
Earth	Sky
Winter	Summer
Yin	Yang
Boaz	Jachin
Low tide	High tide
Waning moon	Waxing moon
Dreaming	Waking
Death	Rebirth

Add your own:

Polarities of Male and Female

Desire | Desired

Gender Morphology

Gender Identity

Gender Expression

Add your own:

References

Abrams, Mere. "Gender Essentialism Is Flawed—Here's Why." *Healthline.* Last medically reviewed on January 27, 2020. https://www.healthline.com/health/gender-essentialism.

Aburrow, Yvonne. "Polarity, Gender, and Fertility." *Dowsing for Divinity.* January 1, 2018, https://dowsingfordivinity.com/2018/01/01/polarity-gender-and-fertility/.

Ainsworth, Thomas. "Form vs. Matter." *The Stanford Encyclopedia of Philosophy* (Summer 2020). https://plato.stanford.edu/archives/sum2020/entries/form-matter.

Alder, Over. "Understanding Polarity in the 21st Century." *Wiccan Rede: Magazine for Wicca and Modern Witchcraft.* January 31, 2016. http://wiccanrede.org/2016/01/understanding-polarity-in-the-21st-century/.

Anonymous [Mary Anne Atwood]. *A Suggestive Inquiry into the Hermetic Mystery.* London: Trelawney Saunders, 1850.

Ariel, David S. *The Mystic Quest: An Introduction to Jewish Mysticism.* Lanham, MD: Rowman & Littlefield, 2004.

Berg, Wendy, and Mike Harris. *Polarity Magic: The Secret History of Western Religion.* St. Paul, MN: Llewellyn, 2003.

Bierlein, J. F. *Parallel Myths.* New York: Ballantine Wellspring, 1994.

Block, Sam. "Hermeticism FAQ: Part 1, Overview and History." The Digital Ambler. June 17, 2021. https://digitalambler.com/2021/06/17/hermeticism-faq-part-i-overview-and-history/.

Bonewits, Isaac. "Pagan Men, Unite!" *Witches & Pagans.* Reprinted from *newWitch* 14 (Spring 2007). https://witchesandpagans.com/opinion/238-pagan-men-unite-nw14.html.

Book, Enfys J. *Queer Qabala: Nonbinary, Genderfluid, Omnisexual Mysticism & Magick.* Woodbury, MN: Llewellyn, 2022.

Chanek, Jack. *Qabalah for Wiccans: Ceremonial Magic on the Pagan Path.* Woodbury, MN: Llewellyn, 2021.

Chapel, Nicholas E. "The Kybalion's New Clothes: An Early 20th Century Text's Dubious Association with Hermeticism." *Journal of the Western Mystery Tradition* 24 (Vernal Equinox 2013). http://www.jwmt.org/v3n24/chapel.html.

Choi, Charles Q., and Scott Dutfield. "7 Theories on the Origin of Life." Live Science. February 14, 2022. https://www.livescience.com/13363-7-theories-origin-life.html.

Crowley, Aleister. *Annotated Liber XV (Book 15) O.T.O.* Hermetic Library. Accessed September 2022. https://hermetic.com/crowley/libers/lib15-annotated.

———. *777 and Other Qabalistic Writings of Aleister Crowley.* San Francisco, CA: Weiser Books, 1986.

Denisoff, Dennis. "The Hermetic Order of the Golden Dawn, 1888–1901." BRANCH: Britain, Representation, and Nineteenth-Century History. Accessed September 2022. http://www.branchcollective.org/?ps_articles=dennis-denisoff-the-hermetic-order-of-the-golden-dawn-1888-1901.

DuQuette, Lon Milo. *The Magick of Aleister Crowley: A Handbook of Rituals of Thelema.* York Beach, ME: Weiser Books, 2003.

Eliot, Alexander. *The Universal Myths: Heroes, Gods, Tricksters and Others.* New York: Meridian, 1990.

Eller, Cynthia. *The Myth of Matriarchal Prehistory: Why an Invented Past Will Not Give Women a Future*. Boston, MA: Beacon Press, 2001.

Ellwood, Taylor, and Lupa. "Polarity in Sex Magick" Spiral Nature Magazine. July 2, 2006. https://www.spiralnature.com/magick/polarity/.

European Society of Endocrinology. "Transgender Brains Are More Like Their Desired Gender from an Early Age." ScienceDaily. May 24, 2018. www.sciencedaily.com/releases/2018/05/180524112351.htm.

Farrar, Janet and Stewart. *A Witches' Bible: The Complete Witches' Handbook*. Custer, WA: Phoenix, 1996. Note that this book combines two earlier books: *Eight Sabbats for Witches* (1981) and *The Witches' Way* (1984). Page numbering in *A Witches' Bible* preserves the original—that is, it restarts from page 1 in the second half.

———. *The Witches' Way: Principles, Rituals and Beliefs of Modern Witchcraft*. London: Robert Hale, 1984.

Fortune, Dion. *The Cosmic Doctrine*. York Beach, ME: Samuel Weiser, 2000.

———. *The Esoteric Philosophy of Love and Marriage*. Wellingborough, Northamptonshire, England: The Aquarian Press, 1988.

———. *The Mystical Qabalah*. San Francisco, CA: Weiser Books, 2000.

———. *The Sea Priestess*. York Beach, ME: Samuel Weiser, 1978.

Fradenburg, Louise Olga, ed. *Women & Sovereignty*. Edinburgh: Edinburgh University Press, 1992.

Gardner, Gerald Brousseau. *The Meaning of Witchcraft*. New York: Magickal Childe, 1991. First published 1959 by Rider & Co.

———. *Witchcraft Today*. New York: Magickal Childe, 1991. First published in 1954 by Rider & Co.

Garry, John. "What It Really Means to Identify as Two-Spirit in Indigenous Culture." Matador Network. September 21, 2020. https://matadornetwork.com/read/two-spirit-indigenous-culture/.

Golas, Thaddeus. *The Lazy Man's Guide to Enlightenment*. Palo Alto, CA: The Seed Center, 1972.

Gordon, Sib. James. "Gender Is Not a Zero-Sum Game." Thelemic Union. August 24, 2019. https://thelemicunion.com/gender-is-not-a-zero-sum -game/.

Greer, Mary K. "Source of *The Kybalion* in Anna Kingsford's Hermetic System." Mary K. Greer's Tarot Blog. October 8, 2009. https://marykgreer .com/2009/10/08/source-of-the-kybalion-in-anna-kingsford's-hermetic -system/.

———. *Women of the Golden Dawn: Rebels and Priestesses*. Rochester, VT: Park Street Press, 1995.

Hammer, Rabbi Jill. *Return to the Place: The Magic, Meditation, and Mystery of Sefer Yetzirah*. Teaneck, NJ: Ben Yehuda Press, 2020.

Harary, Keith, and Pamela Weintraub. *Lucid Dreams in 30 Days: The Creative Sleep Program*. New York: St. Martin's Press, 1989.

Harrington, Lee. *Sacred Kink: The Eightfold Paths of BDSM and Beyond*. Anchorage, AK: Mystic Productions Press, 2009, 2016.

———, and Tai Fenix Kulystin, eds. *Queer Magic: Power Beyond Boundaries*. Anchorage, AK: Mystic Productions Press, 2018.

Herdt, Gilbert, editor. *Third Sex, Third Gender: Beyond Sexual Dimorphism in Culture and History*. New York: Zone Books, 1994.

Heselton, Philip. *Witchfather: A Life of Gerald Gardner, Volume 2—From Witch Cult to Wicca*. Loughborough, Leicestershire: Thoth Publications, 2012.

Huard, Adrienne. "The Land Is Liminal." Atmos. June 17, 2021. https:// atmos.earth/queer-two-spirit-indigenous-identities/.

IMDb. "About a Boy (2002): Hugh Grant: Will Freeman." Accessed September 2022. https://www.imdb.com/title/tt0276751/characters /nm0000424.

Jung, Carl G. *Psychology and Alchemy*. Volume 12 of the Collected Works of C. G. Jung. Edited and translated by Gerhard Adler and R. F. C. Hull. Princeton, NJ: Princeton University Press, 1968.

Kaczynski, Richard. *Perdurabo: The Life of Aleister Crowley*. Revised and expanded 2nd edition. Berkeley, CA: North Atlantic Books, 2010.

Knece, Hinch. "Who Were the Harvey Girls?" Grand Canyon National Park Lodges. March 1, 2020. https://www.grandcanyonlodges.com /connect/who-were-the-harvey-girls/.

Kraig, Donald Michael. *Modern Sex Magick: Secrets of Erotic Spirituality.* St. Paul, MN: Llewellyn, 1998.

Landstreet, Lynna. "Alternate Currents: Revisioning Polarity; or, What's a Nice Dyke Like You Doing in a Polarity-Based Tradition Like This?" Wild Ideas. 1993. http://www.wildideas.net/temple/library/altcurrents.html.

Laqueur, Thomas. *Making Sex: Body and Gender from the Greeks to Freud.* Cambridge, MA: Harvard University Press, 1990.

Leeming, David Adams. *The World of Myth: An Anthology.* New York: Oxford University Press, 1990.

Lipp, Deborah. *The Beginner's Guide to the Occult: Understanding the History, Key Concepts, and Practices of the Supernatural.* Emeryville, CA: Rockridge Press, 2021.

———. *The Elements of Ritual: Air, Fire, Water & Earth in the Wiccan Circle.* St. Paul, MN: Llewellyn, 2003.

———. *Magical Power for Beginners: How to Raise & Send Energy for Spells That Work.* Woodbury, MN: Llewellyn, 2017.

———. *The Study of Witchcraft: A Guidebook to Advanced Wicca.* San Francisco, CA: Red Wheel/Weiser, 2007.

———. *The Way of Four: Create Element Balance in Your Life.* St. Paul, MN: Llewellyn, 2004.

Madeleine. "What Were the 12 Labors of Hercules?" Theoi Greek Mythology. September 13, 2019. https://www.theoi.com/articles/what -were-the-12-labors-of-hercules/.

Magdalene, Misha. *Outside the Charmed Circle: Exploring Gender & Sexuality in Magical Practice.* Woodbury, MN: Llewellyn, 2020.

Magus Incognito [William Walker Atkinson]. *The Secret Doctrine of the Rosicrucians: A Lost Classic.* San Francisco, CA: Red Wheel/Weiser, 2012. First published by Advanced Thought Publishing Co. in 1918.

Mankey, Jason. *Transformative Witchcraft: The Greater Mysteries*. Woodbury, MN: Llewellyn, 2019.

Merriam-Webster. "Can 'Other' Be Used as a Verb?" Accessed September 2022. https://www.merriam-webster.com/words-at-play/other-as-a-verb.

Minai, Thista. *Casting a Queer Circle: Non-Binary Witchcraft*. Hubbardston, MA: Asphodel Press, 2017.

Monaghan, Patricia. *The Book of Goddesses & Heroines*. St. Paul, MN: Llewellyn, 1990.

Montañez, Amanda. "Beyond XX and XY: The Extraordinary Complexity of Sex Determination." Scientific American. September 1, 2017. https://www.scientificamerican.com/article/beyond-xx-and-xy-the-extraordinary-complexity-of-sex-determination/.

Moriarty, Theodore W. C. *The Mystery of Man*. Southall, UK: Blackburn Business Services, 1976.

MSNBC. "Transcript: The Rachel Maddow Show, November 19, 2020." November 19, 2020. https://www.msnbc.com/transcripts/transcript-rachel-maddow-show-november-19-2020-n1260618.

Neal, Brandi. "A New Study Shows Why Bisexual People May Have Higher Rates of Depression." Bustle. April 22, 2019. https://www.bustle.com/p/bisexual-people-have-higher-rates-of-depression-for-these-reasons-a-large-new-study-suggests-17133630.

Open Ocean Exploration (@RebeccaRHelm). "Friendly neighborhood biologist here. I see a lot of people are talking about biological sexes and gender right now…." Twitter thread, December 19, 2019, 7:25 p.m. https://twitter.com/RebeccaRHelm/status/1207834357639139328.

Owen, Alex. *The Place of Enchantment: British Occultism and the Culture of the Modern*. Chicago, IL: University of Chicago Press, 2004.

Patai, Raphael. *The Hebrew Goddess*. Detroit, MI: Wayne State University Press, 1990.

———. *The Jewish Alchemists: A History and Source Book*. Princeton, NJ: Princeton University Press, 2014.

Perlman, Merrill. "How the Word 'Queer' Was Adopted by the LGBTQ Community." Columbia Journalism Review. January 22, 2019, https://www.cjr.org/language_corner/queer.php.

Pitzl-Waters, Jason. "Gender, Transgender, Politics, and Our Beloved Community." *The Wild Hunt*. Patheos. February 27, 2012. https://www.patheos.com/blogs/wildhunt/2012/02/gender-transgender-politics-and-our-beloved-community.html.

Pollack, Rachel. *Doom Patrol #70*. New York: DC Comics/Vertigo, 1993.

Rabin, Nathan. "The Bataan Death March of Whimsy Case File #1: *Elizabethtown*." *The A.V. Club*. January 25, 2007. https://www.avclub.com/the-bataan-death-march-of-whimsy-case-file-1-elizabet-1798210595.

Richardson, Alan. *20th Century Magic and the Old Religion: Dion Fortune, Christine Hartley, Charles Seymour*. St. Paul, MN: Llewellyn, 1991.

Robinson, Tasha. "Dan Savage." The A.V. Club. February 8, 2006. https://www.avclub.com/dan-savage-1798308285.

Rolleston, T. W. *Celtic Myths and Legends*. New York: Dover, 1990.

Schnitker, Sarah A., and Robert A. Emmons. "Hegel's Thesis-Antithesis-Synthesis Model." In *Encyclopedia of Sciences and Religions*, edited by Anne L. C. Runehov and Lluis Oviedo. Dordrecht, Germany: Springer, 2013. doi.org/10.1007/978-1-4020-8265-8_200183.

Seitz, Matt Zoller. "The Offensive Movie Cliche That Won't Die." Salon. September 14, 2010. https://www.salon.com/2010/09/14/magical_negro_trope/.

Sledge, Dr. Justin. "Kabbalah + Alchemy + Magic – The Refiner's Fire – אש מצרף – Transmutation & Jewish Mystical Theurgy." *Esoterica*. YouTube video, February 5, 2021. https://youtu.be/lqLe7HVdhqc.

Sun, Simón(e) D. "Stop Using Phony Science to Justify Transphobia." Scientific American. June 13, 2019. https://blogs.scientificamerican.com/voices/stop-using-phony-science-to-justify-transphobia/.

Three Initiates. *The Kybalion: A Study of the Hermetic Philosophy of Ancient Egypt and Greece*. Chicago, IL: The Yogi Publication Society, 1908.

———. *The Kybalion.* 1912. Accessed September 2022. https://www
.sacred-texts.com/eso/kyb/index.htm.

Valiente, Doreen. *An ABC of Witchcraft.* Custer, WA: Phoenix Publishing,
1973.

———. "The Charge of the Goddess." DoreenValiente.org. Accessed
September 2022. https://www.doreenvaliente.com/doreen-valiente
-Doreen_Valiente_Poetry-11.php.

———. *The Rebirth of Witchcraft.* London: Robert Hale, 1989.

———. *Witchcraft for Tomorrow.* London: Robert Hale, 1978.

Wakefield, Lily. "This Is How Many LGBT People Identify as Asexual in
America." Pink News. August 9, 2019. https://www.pinknews.co.uk
/2019/08/09/how-many-lgbt-people-identify-asexual-america/.

Walker, Valerie "Feri FAQ." Feri: American Traditional Witchcraft. August
2008. http://www.feritradition.org/faq.html.

Williams, Brandy. *The Woman Magician: Revisioning Western Metaphysics from
a Woman's Perspective and Experience.* Woodbury, MN: Llewellyn, 2011.

Wolkstein, Diane, and Samuel Noah Kramer. *Inanna, Queen of Heaven and
Earth: Her Stories and Hymns from Sumer.* New York: Harper & Row, 1983.

Woodroffe, Sir John. *S'akti and S'ākta.* 1965; reprint, Chennai, India:
Ganesh & Co., 2010.

Index

To Write to the Author

If you wish to contact the author or would like more information about this book, please write to the author in care of Llewellyn Worldwide Ltd. and we will forward your request. Both the author and the publisher appreciate hearing from you and learning of your enjoyment of this book and how it has helped you. Llewellyn Worldwide Ltd. cannot guarantee that every letter written to the author can be answered, but all will be forwarded. Please write to:

Deborah Lipp
℅ Llewellyn Worldwide
2143 Wooddale Drive
Woodbury, MN 55125-2989
Please enclose a self-addressed stamped envelope for reply,
or $1.00 to cover costs. If outside the U.S.A., enclose
an international postal reply coupon.

Many of Llewellyn's authors have websites with additional information and resources. For more information, please visit our website at http://www.llewellyn.com.

Notes

Notes

Notes

Notes